CONTENTS

Questions That Changed My Life	1
Introduction	2
How To Use This Book	10
Journal Download	19
KNOW THYSELF	20
What's The Most Important Thing To Me?	21
If This Was The Last Time, What Would I Do?	23
What's My True Treasure?	25
What Needs To Have Happened In 3 Years?	26
What Do I Want To Avoid?	27
Am I Being True To Myself?	29
How Do I Want To Show Up In The World?	31
What Does This Action Say?	33
What's My Expectation?	34
How Is My Sense Of Self-Worth Being Defined?	36
Am I Letting My Happiness Be Defined By Someone Else?	38
What Are My Self-Limiting Beliefs?	40
What Are My Triggers?	41
What Lessons Do I Keep Relearning?	42
REACTION	43
How Does This Help Me?	44

How Can I Make This A Win?	47
How Can I Make This An Empowering Story?	49
How Can I Delay My Reaction?	53
Will I Regret This Tomorrow?	55
Why Am I Unhappy?	57
Why Is This Painful?	59
DECISIONS	61
If I Truly Love Myself, Is This Something I Would Do?	62
What Would X Person Do?	64
Is This Decision Reversible?	66
What Are The Consequences?	68
What Are The Emotions Involved Here?	69
If I Could Reverse Any 3 Decisions, Then What?	73
What's The Downside?	75
Is There Asymmetry Here?	78
How Do I Invert This?	80
What Am I Missing?	84
What Are The Controllables Here?	85
How Do I Know What I Know?	87
How Close Am I To This?	89
What Are The Incentives?	94
What's the Path of Hardship Here?	95
How Can I Learn From My Decisions Over Time?	97
MINDFULNESS	99
Why Do I Have This Thought?	100
Does This Thought Deserve To Be Here?	101
Does This Energize Me?	106
What's The Purpose Here?	107

Am I Prepared For This?	110
Is It Controllable?	115
Is This Really Necessary?	117
PERSPECTIVE	118
Does It Work?	119
Am I Entitled To Have An Opinion On This?	120
Will My Idea Change In 10 Years?	123
What Are My Blind Spots?	126
What's Surprising?	127
What Am I Afraid Of?	129
Which One Of Those Am I Dealing With?	131
Is It Signal Or Noise?	133
What's The Low Hanging Fruit Here?	136
RELATIONSHIPS	138
How Can I Make My Relationship Even More Beautiful?	139
Why Have I Invited This Person Into My Life?	140
Where's My Tribe?	142
Do I Surround Myself With Inspiring People?	144
Why Am I Judging?	146
What Else Could This Mean?	148
Am I Attached?	150
Who Do I Trust?	153
Am I In The Right Relationship?	155
PLAY	158
What's The One Thing?	159
What's One Powerful Belief That I need To Adopt Today?	161
What's One Thing I Need To Stop Doing Immediately?	163
Who Do I Need To Be To Do This?	164

What Am I Trying To Avoid?	166
Is This Binary Or Continuous?	168
How Can I Make This Feel Easy?	170
What Should I Be Tracking?	172
How Can I Do This Right?	175
How Can I Do This Better?	177
How Can I Do This Differently?	179
How Can I Do This Bigger?	181
Where Do I Have Leverage?	184
Am I Operating Within My Zone of Genius?	187
How Do I Deserve This?	188
Which Fire Do I Allow To Continue Burning?	190
How Can I Overcome This?	192
What's The True Cost Of This?	193
How Can I Leave The World A Better Place?	195
What Are The Most Important Questions?	196
Conclusion	198

QUESTIONS THAT CHANGED MY LIFE

Rui Zhi Dong © 2023

© Copyright 2023 by Rui Zhi Dong - All Rights Reserved

INTRODUCTION

My journey with questions started one summer morning in 2017 while I was sitting at La Colombe Coffee Roasters in SoHo, New York, sipping my favorite pourover coffee. I was running an eCommerce business at the time, selling electronic accessories on Amazon. Still slightly groggy from the previous night out on the town, I was reading Nassim Taleb's book, *Fooled By Randomness*, and found myself suddenly energized and fascinated by his take on asymmetric payoffs. He organized his career in such a way where he would gain explosive profits from rare events when they occurred. During the times when nothing happened, which of course was *most* of the time, he was losing money. But because the bets were so cheap, it was still incredibly profitable and the events happened far more often than what the financial markets were predicting.

When I read about this, I thought, *where in my life are there asymmetric payoffs? Where can I make bets over and over again very cheaply yet have potentially massive gains?* I found the answer in my business where for each new product that I introduced on Amazon (my bet), it would cost anywhere between $1,000 to $14,000. Sometimes they worked out and sold extremely well. Most of the time, they just flopped.

My downside was fixed. I couldn't lose more than what it cost me to bring the product to market. The potential upside on the other hand was exponential. Some of these products were generating $300,000 to $850,000 per year with incredible profit margins.

The payoffs are clearly skewed to the upside. For every 10 bets that I made, maybe 2 would do extremely well. Once I did the math, I no longer felt bad about "wasting" money on products that flopped which had previously been a mental barrier for me in doubling down on what worked. The other barrier was the fact that it can take up to a year for the products to hit its stride so that it can get ranked on Amazon and gain reviews organically. During this time, there's a lot of uncertainty about what will happen, especially since most products don't do well. It's easy to be confident when you look back at what has *already happened* but of course much more difficult in the moment. I can imagine how emotionally painful it must have been for Taleb to be losing money consistently month after month on bets that were going nowhere. Yet he remained confident as he knew the numbers were always going to work out in his favor in the end. Just as I ultimately came to realize the same conclusion. Armed with this insight, I developed a system with help from my suppliers to dramatically increase the number of bets that I made which catapulted my business to the next level.

After seeing how it was only a simple change in my perspective that led to the transformation of my business, I wondered what other power questions I could ask myself that may lead to transformations in other aspects of my life, whether in my relationships, my personal development, my finances, my decision-making skills, and so on.

I spent one Tuesday morning at a cafe asking myself the question, *Where Else Do I Have Asymmetry In My Life? Where Do I Have Small Downside Costs But Potentially Huge Upside Benefits?* I spent about an hour thinking and journaling on this question. I would have this question at the back of my mind during the rest of the week.

One of the answers was reaching out to people I found inspiring. I thought back to 2013 when I emailed Andrew Warner, the host of Mixergy who used credit cards to start a business which later grew into a $30 million a year business. To my surprise, he invited me for scotch at his office.

> Andrew Warner ▮▮▮▮▮▮▮▮ via gmail.com   Wed, Jul 10, 2013, 3:32 AM
> to me
> SF near embarcadero.
>
> Want to come to Mixergy HQ for scotch on Thursday @ 6pm?
>
> How to get on my calendar and through our security:

Of course, I accepted his invitation and had a blast. I met other incredibly interesting people at his office as well during "whisky night" who ended up introducing me to even more people that became my closest friends and remain so to this day.

All it took was for a single email to transform my personal relationships.

I then asked myself, *Who do I find inspiring? Who do I want to meet?* I felt a resistance. A fear. *What am I afraid of?* Rejection. *What's the worst that can happen?* They'd say no. *And then what?* Well... that was pretty much it. I would eventually get over my fear of rejection.

Once I finally had some real money, I found myself naturally drawn to questions about what I actually want out of life. *What's the ideal life that I want to craft? What's the thing that really excites me? What is my purpose? How do I want to spend my time? Who do I want to spend time with? Who do I no longer want to spend my time with? How do I want to show up in the world? How do I want to contribute to the world?* These questions took me on a journey of self-exploration. I wound up in Medellin, Colombia, a beautiful city surrounded by mountains where I spent most of my time reading, journaling, hanging out with friends, doing yoga and hiking. It was a very relaxing and joyful 5 months. It was also the first time that I was able to really step back from the business and think about my life. I realized at this point just how lucky I was to be surrounded by people I love, to be able to spend time exactly how I want to, eat amazing food and a daily routine that helped me get into good shape after years of being heavily overweight. It also gave me space to think about the bigger picture.

It seemed that while I loved starting and growing businesses, at a certain level when it becomes more about managing a big team, it no longer excited me. But it took me a long time to reach that conclusion. I had my ego and identity so closely wrapped up with the idea of being an "entrepreneur," a "successful business owner," that I was unconsciously deluding myself into thinking that I loved what I was doing even though my heart was no longer in it.

When I finally asked myself, *Am I being true to myself?* I already knew that the answer was a definitive no. I just wasn't having fun anymore and it was time to move on.

It seemed clear to me that what I really want to be doing is to follow my intellectual curiosities wherever they may take me, to write, to share my work, and to hopefully make a positive impact along the way. I realized that whether these activities made me a lot of money was secondary. What I wanted was to enjoy my life, have some fun and only do the things that I truly love alongside the people I truly love.

This led me on a journey where I continually sought the better question.

Questions such as:

What if I'm doing this wrong? Am I missing something? Am I happy in this job/career/relationship? Am I hiding something from myself? What's the unasked question here?

I became obsessed with the thoughts in my head.

After all, the mental chatter that's happening inside of your head is essentially just *questions* and answers. I've always thought of our mental real estate to be the most precious one we have.

I discovered that it's far easier to change the narratives inside my head by consistently asking better questions.

By changing your questions, you are effectively changing the conversation inside of your head and, by extension, your life too. After all, **your thoughts are you.** It is by far the most powerful influence in your life. As the ancient Stoic Marcus Aurelius tells us, *the happiness of your life depends upon the quality of your thoughts.* The author Tony Robbins adds that the *quality of your life is a direct reflection of the quality of the questions you are asking yourself.*

Self-defeating thoughts lead to self-defeating emotions, actions and outcomes. Empowering thoughts lead to empowering emotions, actions and outcomes.

Given the importance of thoughts, why would we ever choose to have anything other than the absolute best thoughts so that we may experience the absolute best quality life for ourselves?

If only it were so easy to just replace our thoughts with positive words and affirmation. This is neither easy nor natural. Simply saying to yourself, *I'm rich, I look fabulous, I'm so happy*, over and over again, while hearing your unbelieving mind respond with, *Um, no you're not*, is not likely to be effective.

With powerful questions, you can slowly but permanently shift your inner-dialogue.

When you catch a self-defeating thought, you can start shifting the conversation by asking yourself, *Does this thought deserve to be here? How can I make this an empowering thought? If I can choose* any thoughts to populate my mind, what would they be? How does this help me?

Questions can help us avoid doing stupid things that in retrospect seem rather obvious.

For example, ask yourself, *If I Could Reverse Any 3 Financial Decisions, Then How Much Money Would I Have?*

You'd be surprised at the answer including from the most well respected financial professionals. That's no accident. We all have major blind spots and cognitive biases that prevents us from making rational decisions at times.

Just asking questions can help provide distance to a heated situation, diffuse emotions and prevent decisions we might later come to regret. *What Are The Emotions Involved Here? Will I Regret This Tomorrow?*

Whenever I see poor decision making in myself and in others, I use the opportunity to ask myself, *What Questions Could Have Prevented This?* The investor Charlie Munger likes to say, *All I want to know is where I'm going to die so I'll never go there.* The right questions can help you gain sharp clarity when dealing with a challenging situation. Questions like, *What's The Downside? What Am I Missing? What Are The Incentives?*

Better questions means better insights, better thinking, and ultimately better decision making. Effective organizations build insightful questions into their process.

Having great questions is far more useful than only having great answers.

Questions can be used as a tool for greater self-awareness and to better understand yourself.

Why am I triggered by this? Am I attached? Why do I feel pain?

Changing the questions we ask can empower us and reframe the way we look at situations.

Instead of, *Why Am I Not Rich?* ask, *How Do I Deserve To Become Rich?*
Instead of, *Why Don't I Have My Dream Partner?* ask, *How Do I Deserve My Dream Partner?*

The ability to ask great questions is a profoundly powerful tool.

However, like any other skill, **we need regular practice to get good at it**. To be intentional and thoughtful about the questions we ask.

Keep working at finding the better questions over time and your "questions muscle" will slowly but surely grow stronger, and you will enjoy a valuable lifelong skill that will have a tremendously positive impact on your life.

HOW TO USE THIS BOOK

Consider this your companion thinking and reflection book.

Look at the list of questions and then **choose the questions that resonate the most with you.** I certainly don't expect you to click with *all* of the questions. You can highlight the ones that you want to think about.

Over time, you might find that the questions that resonate with you change, as you yourself go through changes.

Some questions are very situation specific while others are big picture thinking.

Some questions are for asking regularly such as, *Why Do I Have This Thought? Does This Thought Deserve To Be Here? How Can I Make This An Empowering Question? How Can I Make This An Empowering Story? What's The Better Question Here?*

Developing the habit of asking such questions can be enormously beneficial. They have made me much more aware of my thought patterns and I highly recommend asking such questions **throughout the day**.

You can write out the questions for asking regularly on index cards or on post it notes and have them laying around so that you are often reminded of the questions.

Thoughts As A Trigger

You can choose to create *thought triggers* to help you rewire your thought patterns.

For example, if I catch myself thinking, *Why can't I get anything done right??* Then this automatically triggers the question, *How Can I Make This An Empowering Question? How Would I Rephrase The Same Question If I Truly Loved Myself?*

Of course, your mind may resist such questions initially. It wants to continue to wallow. That's okay. The key is just to be **persistent**. Gently, but firmly, repeat the question to yourself.

The first answer might be a weak one. Your brain gives any answer just to get the question over and done with so that it can go back to its negative but familiar thought patterns. *This is silly. It will never work. I'm tired of this stupid questions stuff.*

Keep on asking. *How Can I Make This An Empowering Question?*

Don't stop until your brain takes the question seriously and gives you an answer that you yourself are surprised with.

Once that happens, give yourself a pat on the back :)

Don't be discouraged if it takes some time and many attempts.

Sometimes your mind just needs space to process the question. Remember to stay kind to yourself during this process.

You can also try changing up the questions. *What would X person do? How have I produced Y results previously? How did I get so good at it?*

Take note of the thoughts, how you felt, the questions you used, and write down any observations you've made.

You'll find that some questions work better for particular thoughts and feelings. Keep note of them so that you know which questions are more effective.

For example, "self-doubt triggers X question."

Eventually, your thought patterns will start to shift and you'll notice a positive change in your mood and energy levels too!

Quality Thinking Time

For the bigger questions, consider scheduling "thinking time" on a regular basis where you can be alone with your thoughts and explore the question deeply.

Far too many people get weighed down in doing, and never take the time to think and feel. Take five minutes, an hour, a day, or even a holiday. If you free up some time to think freely, you'll be able to see the bigger picture much easier. — Richard Branson

In our hyper-connected world, it's almost unheard of to spend time just **sitting and thinking.** Yet the benefits and insights that such dedicated reflection time yields are enormous. Warren Buffett, the famed investor, once said, *I insist on a lot of time being spent, almost every day, to just sit and think.* This is the CEO of one the largest companies in the world talking. The idea of a CEO spending his working day just sitting and thinking is highly unorthodox for any Fortune 500 companies, let alone one that's in the top 10. Nonetheless, it's exactly his sitting and thinking that enables Buffett to create immense value for his shareholders by way of his insights.

It's easy to get drawn into the hustle and bustle of life, with its flurry of activity that leaves no space for **quality thinking.** It's easy to confuse keeping our mind stimulated for learning or progress; to obscure the difference between what is noise and what is signal. Bill Gates commented that, *sitting and thinking may be a much higher priority than a normal CEO, where there's all these demands and you feel like you need to go and see all these people. It's not a proxy of your seriousness that you fill every minute in your schedule.*

One way to get started is to schedule 30-40 minutes per week, per fortnight, or per month of dedicated thinking time, with a question chosen from this book that you want to reflect on.

Use this time to just sit still.

To pause and reflect.

Do this in an environment that you find relaxing so that your body and mind can also be in a state of relaxation. I like to keep it simple and just take pen and paper with me to the park or a cozy cafe (along with this book, of course!). Something about using pen and paper makes me feel more connected with my thoughts and seeing my handwriting on paper feels more personal than writing on a laptop. My rule when I do this exercise is no smartphones, no laptops, no distractions, no interruptions.

I find it best to start in the morning before being inundated with any stimulus. If I'm doing this exercise in the afternoon or evening, then I'll meditate first to reset.

For questions that require creative brainstorming, it can be more effective writing in bullet points during my stream of consciousness writing.

Try to write as much as you can. Don't judge, overthink, analyze or try to process your thoughts. And certainly don't put any pressure on yourself.

You can later filter what you've written down and mark the things that you find valuable. You can come back to your notes and add ideas as they pop up, which they often do when you're mind is still working on the question in the background while you're showering or going for a walk.

For certain questions, you may want to intentionally let your unconscious mind chew on it for a while as it continues to look for answers.

Dedicated reflection times are a great opportunity to zoom out and consider questions that you don't normally think about in your day to day life. To make sure that you don't miss the bigger picture and spend life only going through the motions.

What Are The Low Hanging Fruits? Do I Have The Right People In My Life? Am I Working On The Right Things? Am I In The Right Place? Is There Anything Major I Need to Change? What Major Question or Issue Am I Avoiding? What Am I Missing? What's The Most Important Thing To Me?

The more hours I devote to quiet, intense, uninterrupted thinking time, the more **gold nuggets** I get. But unless I put it on the calendar, I just don't do it even when I know how useful this exercise is. Find a system that works for you so that you can commit to investing in yourself on a regular basis.

If you do nothing except **adopt this one habit of regular reflection**, I'll have considered this book having accomplished its goal!

Unleash The Power of Your Mind

What are the questions that you will want to come back to over and over again? Questions that you want your beautiful mind to work on, not just in one sitting but over the months and years?

Given enough time, your brain will work creatively on your

questions and come up with brilliant solutions that will astonish you. And quite often, **just one single creative thought is all you need to get what you want in life**.

Richard Feynman, the Nobel-Prize winning physicist, used a dozen open questions for making breakthrough contributions in science that has made him one of the most important thinkers of our time.

Feynman once said in an interview:

You have to keep a dozen of your favorite problems constantly present in your mind, although by and large they will lay in a dormant state. Every time you hear or read a new trick or a new result, test it against each of your twelve problems to see whether it helps. Every once in a while there will be a hit, and people will say, "How did he do it? He must be a genius!"

Tiago Forte, in his book *Building a Second Brain*, writes that, "Feynman's approach encouraged him to follow his interests wherever they might lead. He posed questions and constantly scanned for solutions to long-standing problems in his reading, conversations, and everyday life. When he found one, he could make a connection that looked to others like a flash of unparalleled brilliance."

This can be applied at an organizational level too. Bridgewater Associates, a $140 billion asset manager, built its entire organization over the decades around just two questions:

1. *How does the global economy work?*

2. *How do you take that understanding and utilize it to build great portfolios?*

The question should be an open one and have some **emotional power** for you.

Imagine asking yourself, *How Can I Achieve Financial Independence?* when you don't really care about money and have your heart set on being a monk.

Questions are powerful when it comes from somewhere deep.

These will end up being the questions that you come back to time and again. The questions that will drive your life.

One of my questions is, *How Can I Have More Powerful Thoughts?* I resonate deeply with this question because of my desire to improve the quality of my life through my inner world. That ultimately led to this list of powerful questions for reflection that you now hold in your hands.

A Quick Note On Questions

You can of course use only the questions alone in this book without the accompanying text. They are there in case you want more context for the questions. They represent my perspectives, my beliefs and my biases, and you're certainly free to ignore them as you choose :)

JOURNAL DOWNLOAD

As an owner of this edition of:

51 Questions That Changed My Life

you are entitled to download the *Questions Journal* in PDF format that is DRM-free to use on any eReader, tablet or smartphone.

Simple go to:

https://bit.ly/3CIfPoY

to get your copy now.

KNOW THYSELF

To know thyself is the beginning of wisdom — Socrates

He who knows others is wise. He who knows himself is enlightened. — Lao Tzu

'Seek within - know thyself,' these secret and sublime hints come to us wafted from the breath of Rishis through the dust of ages. — Swami Ramdas

WHAT'S THE MOST IMPORTANT THING TO ME?

Take the opportunity to reflect on what you want in life.

Consider what you want your life to stand for. Your likes and dislikes.

You're not a still image fixed in time and space.

You're a living, breathing creature that's constantly changing, slowly but surely.

No man ever steps in the same river twice. For it's not the same river and he's not the same man. —Heraclitus

What you want, who you want to be, can also change.

Take a moment to revisit your priorities and your values by asking yourself, *What's the most important thing to me?*

This year, the most important things may remain the same.

Another year, it may change.

Sometimes significantly.

And that's fine.

Be aware of what's changed.

Choose to stay true to who you are by accepting and embracing your change.

Even if that means making some unexpected, perhaps painful, life adjustments.

IF THIS WAS THE LAST TIME, WHAT WOULD I DO?

For the past 33 years, I have looked in the mirror every morning and asked myself: 'If today were the last day of my life, would I want to do what I am about to do today?' And whenever the answer has been 'No' for too many days in a row, I know I need to change something.
— Steve Jobs

Think of yourself as dead. You have lived your life. Now take what's left and live it properly. — Marcus Aurelius

Ask yourself, *If this was the last day/week/month/year of my life, would I do what I'm about to do?*

This question can help us look at the bigger picture.

Death helps us focus. It's a reminder that time is not unlimited and it needs to be used wisely.

Memento mori — remember death. Remembering death can help us find the strength and courage to do what we really want. To avoid sleep walking through life and to prioritize the things that are truly important to us.

The more real you make the impending death feel, the more insightful your answers will be.

Spend time visualizing your funeral (a bit dark, I know!)

You might suddenly discover in your visualization that you've been living someone else's dream.

Or just holding back on pursuing something you really want because you're afraid of the risk.

Or not spending enough time with loved ones.

The beautiful thing is that you can start right now while you have time.

WHAT'S MY TRUE TREASURE?

Where your treasure is, there your heart will be also. — Matthew 6:21

Is it money?

Is it relationships?

Is it nature?

Is it a state of mind?

Is it health?

Is it work?

Another related question to consider: *How do I measure success in life?*

WHAT NEEDS TO HAVE HAPPENED IN 3 YEARS?

For this question, imagine yourself in 3 years' time.

You're watching a film reel from the future in your head.

Try to make the film as *vivid* as possible.

Picture your surroundings. *Where are you? What do you smell? What sensations do you feel? What are you working on? Who are you with?*

You're feeling deeply satisfied with where you are and how far you've come.

Now ask yourself, *What needs to have happened between now and then for you to feel satisfied with how you've progressed?*

WHAT DO I WANT TO AVOID?

What do you want to avoid in life?

This can be just as useful, if not more so, than setting big goals and trying to chase after success.

When you single-mindedly pursuing your dreams, you run the risk of missing obvious pitfalls.

These can start from simple things like avoiding toxic people, avoiding an early death (aids, shootings, drugs), avoiding bad relationships, avoiding a bad reputation, and so on.

I try to avoid dealing with people I don't particularly enjoy being around both professionally and personally, avoid having high expectations, avoid drama, excess, envy, and working on anything I don't love.

Create a list of the all the things you want to avoid. It can also include behavior that turns you off, the kind of situations that you want to avoid, and so on. This list can also serve as a useful guide for adjusting your own behavior whenever you catch yourself doing something that you don't like in others.

It's also easier to figure out what you *don't want to do* than figuring out what you *do want to do*.

Start with the low hanging fruit and list out all the things we don't want in our life by asking, *What Do I Want To Avoid?*

AM I BEING TRUE TO MYSELF?

We are all unique in some way.

We have our own nature.

Our own rhythms and our own journey in life.

It can be difficult to see when we're subject to daily conditioning about how we *should* be.

Small signals that you download all around you in your environment — from your family, your school, your friends, your colleagues, and so on. *You should strive to be wealthy. You should strive to be beautiful. You should strive to be popular. You should strive to have a successful career.*

Ask yourself, *Am I Being True To Myself?*

Don't focus on what others say, or what they expect you to be.

Choose instead to trust your inner core.

Express your individuality.

Accentuate your differences.

Stop comparing or measuring yourself to other people's standards.

Be truly proud to be who *you* are.

Even if it comes out very differently to what others or even you yourself had expected.

HOW DO I WANT TO SHOW UP IN THE WORLD?

Withdraw into yourself and look. And if you do not find yourself beautiful yet, act as does the creator of a statue that is to be made beautiful: he cuts away here, he smoothes there, he makes this line lighter, this other purer, until a lovely face has grown upon his work. So do you also: [...] never cease chiselling your statue. — Plotinus

Think about the people that inspire you. How do they behave? What are the traits that you admire most about them? Reflect on this and write a list. Is it their generosity? Their courage?

Here are a few more qualities:
- Integrity
- Honesty
- Confidence
- Patience
- Persistence
- Self-Respect

Now think about the people that turn you off. What is it about them turns you off? Is it their attitude? That they take shortcuts? Their dishonesty? Their greed? Whatever you come up with, write them down.

Once you have your list, think about how you might work each day trying to behave more like the people you admire and less like the ones you don't.

WHAT DOES THIS ACTION SAY?

The first principle is that you must not fool yourself, and you are the easiest person to fool. — Richard Feynman

May the outward and inward man be at one. — Plato

There are times when we tell ourselves (and others) one thing and our actions say the exact *opposite*.

Pay attention when it happens.

When the same incongruence happens often, consider them useful clues.

You can say that you love someone, but then never make time to see that person.

You can say that you love your job, but feel your stomach churn at the sight of the office.

Ask yourself, *What Is My Action Really Trying To Say? How Can I Explore This Further?*

WHAT'S MY EXPECTATION?

My expectations were reduced to zero when I was 21. Everything since then has been a bonus. — Stephen W. Hawking

Consider the expectations that you hold.

Some are conscious.

You expect your coffee to be served perfectly. You're expecting a 10% raise. For house prices to go up.

Some are unconscious.

You expect your friends, your partner, your colleagues to behave in a certain way. For the comforts of life to always be available instantly.

When reality clashes with expectations, you experience disappointment and unhappiness.

Expectations about things that fall outside of your control can be frustrating.

Focus your energy and efforts instead on things within your control.

Consider the expectations that you're currently holding.

Especially the expectations that cause anxiety.

Happiness doesn't depend on how well things are going.

It depends on how they're going relative to your expectations.

And your expectations are fully within your control.

HOW IS MY SENSE OF SELF-WORTH BEING DEFINED?

Are you letting your sense of self worth be defined by some measure of success?

By what people think of you, your image, or by how much attention you get?

The stronger your sense of self worth is tied to something external, the more your emotions will fluctuate.

The highs come from receiving the validation you crave.

The lows from when your expectations don't get met.

Events outside of your control will always happen.

And your emotions will constantly be in a state of flux.

You can change this by starting with how your self worth is defined.

The person's opinion that should matter the most to you is the person that's staring back at you in the mirror every morning.

Operate by the standards that you've set for yourself and live by your own code of conduct.

Let your self worth flow from your full acceptance and love of self.

AM I LETTING MY HAPPINESS BE DEFINED BY SOMEONE ELSE?

A man cannot be comfortable without his own approval — Mark Twain

It mattered a great deal to me whether someone liked me, whether they thought I was successful, whether they thought that I was smart. I got attached to the idea that I had to be perceived in a particular way and I worked hard to control that image. It took some time to start letting it go.

If a girl I really liked didn't reply to my message, I'd obsess over it. Voices of self doubt would start creeping in. *Maybe I'm not good enough? Maybe I did something wrong? Maybe she sees straight through me and sees all of my inadequacies.* If I became aware of the negative thought loop, I'll snap out of it. If not, I'll obsess for a while, constantly checking the last time they were seen online and mentally listing out all of the possible reasons why they wouldn't reply. Suffice it to say, it was pretty exhausting and not all that productive.

Events outside of your control will always happen. Someone breaks up with you. You get a bad performance review. You get fired. Your business fails. You get bad publicity. Someone ghosts you. You get called an idiot. Shit happens.

How you react to the setback is what counts and it's what you have control over.

WHAT ARE MY SELF-LIMITING BELIEFS?

Beliefs are powerful.

Beliefs drive choices which in turn drives action.

It doesn't matter whether those beliefs are true.

What matters is what you believe.

Before the 4 minute mile was broken, nobody thought it was possible to break it.

After it was broken, it got broken regularly.

You can choose to believe in your own star and your own fortune. Your right to be here and make your mark. Or you can go through life believing that you're not deserving of anything.

What beliefs are holding me back?

What are the cost of those self-limiting beliefs?

WHAT ARE MY TRIGGERS?

Consider the last time that you were triggered.

What were the causes?

What were the underlying issues?

How did it make you feel?

How did you deal with it?

How would you deal with it in the perfect world?

WHAT LESSONS DO I KEEP RELEARNING?

There are some lessons that we just keep learning over and over in life.

Simple things like not using the phone first thing in the morning. Or reacting immediately to someone saying something we find unpleasant.

They can be lessons to achieve good outcomes or to avoid bad results.

If you were to create a list of such lessons to keep yourself from having to relearn the same lessons over and over again, what would be on that list?

The list should be very individual to you.

The specific lessons that you find to be both valuable and useful.

REACTION

When we are no longer able to change a situation, we are challenged to change ourselves — Viktor E. Frankl

HOW DOES THIS HELP ME?

There is nothing either good or bad, but thinking makes it so. — William Shakespeare

Sometimes we experience situations where we spiral.

We know when we're in that state. The trick is to identify those states in the moment and then to use those states as a *trigger* to ask the question, How Does This Help Me?

You know whether you're in a positive or negative state.

Identification usually isn't the hard part. The challenge is having the awareness that you've entered such a state. The shift in states can happen just beneath the surface of consciousness.

It takes a bit of time to train the mind and build up the habit to have those states act as a trigger for asking the right questions.

You can use emotions such as envy, resentment, anger, revenge, self pity as cues for reflection.

Initially it won't feel like it makes much of a difference.

Let's say that you're feeling envious of a close friend that just had a massive business success. You start making comparisons. You feel unworthy. You start to feel some self pity. Your thoughts start to spiral. You suddenly remember to ask yourself, *How Does This Help Me?*

But your mind won't really register the question and hit right back with, "That doesn't matter! It sucks that he gets all this success and credit, and it's not fair. That should be me. I've worked just as hard."

Put everything that you're feeling and thinking onto paper. No judgment. Just let it all flow.

Keep in mind that you're retraining the internal dialogue that's going on and the deep grooves that your brain has developed over the years doesn't just change instantaneously.

But stick with it and you'll start to feel the inner dialogue change and your dips into the negative emotional state will slowly shorten the more you do this.

Just the act of learning to identify the feeling will enable you to catch it earlier once your emotional state starts to shift.

You'll start to notice some similar patterns in thought, feeling or triggers.

I often think about what the UFC fighter, Conor McGregor, once said:

At the end of day, you've got to feel some way.

So why not feel unbeatable?

Why not feel untouchable?

You can choose, right now, to adopt the state that will help you the most; the state that makes you feel *positive, powerful, energetic.*

When you catch yourself starting to drift off, ask yourself, *How Does This Help Me?*

HOW CAN I MAKE THIS A WIN?

Life is 10% what happens to me and 90% of how I react to it. —John C. Maxwell

We will all face adversity.

That's an inescapable fact of life.

How you react to it is within your control.

And therein lies your opportunity.

For example, imagine getting fired and suddenly losing a stable source of income. It will probably feel terribly upsetting in the moment.

Ask yourself, *How Can I Make This A Win?*

Well...

I guess can take this opportunity to reskill.
I now have time to look for a better paid job or a better company.
I can start consulting or a new business.
I can finally take some time off to reflect and figure out my next move.

I can now spend some quality time with my family and friends.
I can change the direction of my career altogether.

This may just turn out to be a blessing in disguise.

Look for the win.

The times when it seems the most difficult or ridiculous to do so is oftentimes when it needs to be done the most.

Not when the win is obvious and you're already celebrating but when it's *hard.*

HOW CAN I MAKE THIS AN EMPOWERING STORY?

The mind is the ultimate story generating machine.

It will look at disconnected dots and create patterns, even when there is none.

It perceives the world through the stories it generates. It's how we can make sense of the world and weave all of the inputs we receive into a picture that we can understand and relate to.

Some of those stories are positive. However, a lot of the stories it generates are also negative and self limiting. These are the ones to watch out for.

The beautiful thing is that you can replace these thoughts with empowering beliefs and stories that you create. That is wholly within your control. You can come up with whatever story you think works best for you.

Whenever you feel yourself starting to descend into negativity, ask yourself, *How Can I Make This An Empowering Story?*

Let's say that you've just started dating and you hear yourself thinking, *This person that I dated thinks that I'm a loser because he stopped replying to my texts a few days ago. That's why he doesn't want to hang out with me. I knew I shouldn't have talked so much during the date. And that dress I wore? I should have chosen something more elegant. He must have thought I looked terrible.*

This thought serves no real purpose and telling yourself this will only keep you suspended in a state of negativity.

Choose a better story.

He must be very busy or he just has low interest which is okay because I'm not going to like every single person that I date and he's not going to like every person that he dates either. That's perfectly natural.

Or, *I want to be with the kind of person that communicates well, states his intention clearly and his behavior demonstrates otherwise. I don't think it's going to work out and I'm going to move on.*

Other dating examples include I'll never find someone like him/her again, I don't deserve him/her.

Now let's say that you're getting started in business. You quit your 9–5 job to start a new venture and you hit a road bump. Maybe you haven't been able to raise the capital you need because you got turned down a few times by investors. Or that you haven't been able to get the sale you need to validate your business model.

As any experienced business person will tell you, that's perfectly normal. But sometimes, the mind will start crafting stories. You're a fraud. You have no idea what you're doing. That's why you're getting rejected. This is never going to work. You shouldn't have even tried this to begin with. What were you thinking. Now you need to see whether you can get your old job back. You're running out of money and you have no income. This is not a good situation to be in.

You can reframe this into an empowering story.

This a numbers game. One person saying no, or 20 people for that matter, doesn't really mean anything. This is a great opportunity for me to practice, learn, and create something I've never done before. What a great learning experience and I'm proud of myself for taking the leap. I'll consider the feedback I get during this process to refine what I do to get better and increase my probabilities of getting what I want.

Pay attention to the stories in your head.

Keep in mind that *everyone* battles at some stage with feelings of not being good enough, feeling like a fraud, feeling that there's something wrong with them, even though it can feel like you're the only one struggling through it at the time.

The key is how you react to the narrative when you catch this thought pattern.

Take a deep breath and ask yourself, *How Can I Make This An Empowering Story?*

Sometimes, it can be a matter of reframing the question itself.

For this, use the question, *How Can I Make This An Empowering Question?*

For example, *Why doesn't he like me?*

We can change this to, *What are things he likes about me?*

Or from, *Why can't things ever just go my way?*

To, *What are things that have worked well for me recently?*

To help you frame the questioning better, imagine changing your inner voice from one of a harsh self-critic to one that's loving, kind and generous.

It will take some time and consistent effort to shift the inner voice.

But it will pay-off in a big way.

HOW CAN I DELAY MY REACTION?

Whenever you encounter an issue or obstacle of some kind, your natural instinct is to solve it as soon as possible. Especially when there's an urgent deadline.

We are emotional and impulsive creatures.

Our minds have been trained to react immediately (fight or flight) to ensure our survival. This makes sense when you're faced with a lion in the jungle and you only have a split second to react.

Thankfully, most situations today are not as time sensitive. We have time to think through different scenarios.

It's a common tactic for sales people to create artificial deadlines to give a false sense of urgency and sometimes it's very effective. In most cases, you do not need to respond immediately

When there's pressure to respond immediately, ask yourself, *What's the worst that can happen if I delay? If I go beyond the deadline?* It's often not as bad as we imagine it to be.

If you're feeling emotional, it's a good time to step back and ask yourself, *How Can I Delay My Reaction?*

The bigger the issue, the more important it is to think first and create some space.

WILL I REGRET THIS TOMORROW?

You know, Warren, you can tell a guy to go to hell tomorrow. You don't give up the right. So just keep your mouth shut today, and see if you feel the same way tomorrow. — Tom Murphy

Think about the last time that you told somebody off. *What was the benefit? Was it worth the cost?*

It might feel good telling another person off in the moment.

But if you're like most people, you'll come to regret losing your temper.

To temper your emotions, take some time to yourself and write down all the things you want to say, point by point.

And if you're feeling the same way the next day, then you can use that material. As Tom Murphy once said, you don't lose your optionality by keeping what you have to say to yourself. You can always tell the guy to go to hell tomorrow.

However, by acting on your impulse in the moment, you've lost your optionality. You can no longer reverse your decision.

When you're in the heat of the moment next, ask yourself, *Will I*

RUI ZHI DONG

Regret This Tomorrow?

WHY AM I UNHAPPY?

Whenever you find yourself feeling annoyed or unhappy about something, look for the **underlying expectation** that caused the feeling.

Naval Ravikant once said that *desire is a contract that you make with yourself to be unhappy until you get what you want.*

Certainly having **high expectations** can help build **great capabilities**.

However, if your expectations and standards are so high such that you *only* allow yourself to be happy when things are going absolutely perfectly... well, it's going to be hard to be happy and grateful.

Choose your battles wisely.

Do you get upset if your coffee doesn't come out the way you like it?

Or maybe because you get cut off in traffic by an idiot that's not paying attention?

Or maybe it turned out to be a rainy day when it was meant to be a nice, sunny day and your plans for doing some fun outdoor activity is ruined?

Your energy is finite.

There will always be something wrong.

And that's fine.

The next time you get triggered, ask yourself, *Why Am I Unhappy?*

Look for the underlying expectation and then decide whether it's a battle worth fighting.

WHY IS THIS PAINFUL?

Pain + Reflection = Progress — Ray Dalio

Facing difficulties is inevitable. Learning from them is optional. — John C. Maxwell

The next time you experience pain, Ask Yourself, *Why Is This Painful?*

Instead of feeling frustrated or overwhelmed by the pain, view it as an opportunity for growth.

Pain is a useful signal that there's something to be learned. The stronger the pain, the more there is to discover.

Certainly it can be challenging to reflect when there's a lot of pain involved.

When you go through pain, remind yourself that you'll have a lot more to gain if you choose to process it instead of burying it. Journaling in the heat of the moment can help take the sting away.

Pain can be a signal to address some issue at work, in your relationship, and so on. It can point to unresolved childhood issues. It can reveal insecurities. It can expose false beliefs. It can illuminate your feelings about death.

Let pain be an emotion that triggers the thought, *Why Is This Painful?*

DECISIONS

I am not a product of my circumstances. I am a product of my decisions. — Stephen Covey

IF I TRULY LOVE MYSELF, IS THIS SOMETHING I WOULD DO?

The goal of this question is to put some distance inside your head between you and your actions so that you can visualize yourself in the third person.

It's a question worth asking yourself, especially when you're hesitating.

You've been seeing a guy for some time and you recently noticed his negativity come out and his tendency to criticize small things about you. Your appearance. How you talk about your work. But he was so sweet at the start. *What to do? Keep seeing him? If I truly loved myself, is this something that I would do?*

Some examples of internal dialogue:

If I truly loved myself, I wouldn't tolerate being treated this way and I've allowed it to go on because I'm afraid of being alone.

Or

If I truly loved myself, I would allow myself to express my emotions honestly and since his criticisms bother me, I'm going to tell him that.

You've been hesitating about your work in law. The money's good. But you've stopped growing sometime ago and the work is no longer fulfilling. Your real passion is architecture but that'd mean going back to school and starting at the bottom. You've got a comfortable life now and you don't want to change that. *If I truly loved myself, is this something that I would do?*

Some examples of internal dialogue:

If I truly loved myself, I would do something that excites me, even if that means drastically downgrading my lifestyle because I would be spending the majority of my working hours on something I love and be true to myself.

Or

If I truly loved myself, I will stick with what I know best and allow myself the certainty of having a high paying salary so that I may enjoy the good life and I can pursue architecture as a hobby.

WHAT WOULD X PERSON DO?

When making decisions, ask yourself, *What Would X Person Do?*

That person would be someone that you're trying to model or that you think would make the best decision in the same situation.

It can be a different person for each domain. You can ask yourself, *Who would the person to make the best decision in this situation?*

You can pick and choose what you admire about the person.

When I think about investment related decisions, that person is Warren Buffett. For personal development, Jim Rohn. For relationships, Esther Perel. For Stoicism, Marcus Aurelius. For quality of life thinking, Ed Thorp.

It can also be a group of people that act like your "mental board of directors" where you get the unique perspectives of each person.

The people on my list is influenced by how much of their work I've "internalized."

I've read and re-read books they've written. Watched their

videos. Written notes. The more you know about the person, the better and more useful this question will be for you.

Purposely read their written work with the intention of understanding how they think. The logic they use. How they have come to their conclusions. Their philosophy.

This can also be someone you know personally — family members, friends, colleagues, teachers, and so on — and something about them that you particularly admire. I have a close friend who stays incredibly calm under intense pressure and doesn't let the pressure impact his ability to think through decisions carefully. He first checks to see whether there's an actual time constraint. Then knowing how much time he has to work with, he'll ask powerful questions to gather the information needed to make an informed decision and figure out what the core issue is. For pretty much every situation, he has an effective way of navigating it, even when it looks like an impossible situation to most. *What are the goals of the people involved? What are the emotions people are feeling? What are the incentives here? How can everybody come out of this feeling satisfied?* Whenever I need to make a decision when emotions are running high, I think about him first.

When making decisions, ask yourself, *What Would X Person Do?*

The additional advantage of asking this question is that you give yourself some space to avoid making emotional decisions so that you get some detachment and you get the opportunity to assess the situation more objectively.

IS THIS DECISION REVERSIBLE?

Before making a decision, ask yourself, *Is This Decision Reversible?*

Jeff Bezos talks about two kinds of decisions.

Type 1 decisions are those that are permanent, irreversible. They're usually large decisions and deserve considerable attention.

Type 2 decisions are reversible. If you buy something on Amazon you don't like, it's easily reversible and you have a long time to change your mind about your purchase. They don't require as much thinking power.

Figure out which type of decision you're dealing with.

If you apply Type 1 thinking indiscriminately to all decisions, then you'll be depleting your decision making bank unnecessarily and sometimes make poorer Type 1 decisions because of decision fatigue. You may even procrastinate on all decision making as result.

By knowing what type of decision you're dealing with, you can give Type 1 decisions the brain power they deserve and make faster decisions when it comes to Type 2 decisions.

The same goes the other way around. If you apply Type 2 thinking to all Type 1 decisions, you'll start to make a lot of bad decisions that will compound over time.

When you identify Type 1 decisions, you can also ask, *How Can I Make This Reversible? What's the Cost? Is It Worth It?*

This exercise can help you become aware of any potential downsides and look to minimize any risks associated with the decision.

Identify the decision type you're dealing with by asking yourself, *Is This Decision Reversible?*

WHAT ARE THE CONSEQUENCES?

We commonly overweigh first-order consequences and ignore second-order and third-order consequences.

It can feel mentally taxing to keep asking, *And what would happen after that? And after that? And after that?*

For some decisions, it's really worth spending the time to zoom out, carefully think through the consequences and consider the knock-on effects a decision can have.

A useful exercise is to imagine that you're watching a movie in your head. You're observing, without judgment or emotion, how events unfold over time for each given decision. Once you've finished watching the different movies, then you can put your analytical hat on and start assessing.

What are the best case consequences and their odds?

What are the worst case consequences and their odds?

Given these, is it worth it?

WHAT ARE THE EMOTIONS INVOLVED HERE?

Simply being aware of what emotions are at work and identifying them *before* you respond is powerful. It helps you detach. It allows you to zoom out. It gives you the space you need to think, and then to *choose* your reaction.

I'm feeling angry. I'm feeling happy. I'm feeling fearful. I'm feeling greedy. I'm feeling sad. I'm feeling unmotivated. I'm feeling hopeful. I'm feeling despair.

Then ask yourself, *What Does That Mean?*

Write it out, even if when it seems very obvious.

I'm feeling angry. It means that I'm probably not going to be thinking clearly and might do something I'll regret.

What Does That Mean?

Maybe it's good to journal on this. Talk it over with a trusted friend. Sleep on it. Exercise.

Emotions can provide us with information.

When our body wants to be fed, it sends us a signal by releasing hormones to trigger the feeling of hunger.

What we do with that signal is up to us. If we're fasting, then we can dismiss the signal and eat later.

We can do the same with emotions. Let's say that we start feeling fearful. From our hunter-gatherer days, fear signified the need to flee. Fear signals danger. Today, we can analyze the alert and determine whether there's real danger involved. If there's no real danger involved, we can put aside the alert.

By recognizing our emotions, we can observe the ebb and flow without attachment. We can choose our response.

This opens us up to empathize more deeply with others when we're not subject to our own internal chaos.

In group situations, say during a negotiation, you can take a bird's-eye perspective by asking yourself the same question, *What Are The Emotions Involved Here?*

This will give you the opportunity to closely observe all of the parties, consider their individual circumstances and what emotions their circumstances may trigger. You can then decide the best way to approach the conversation.

If negotiations has dragged on *far longer* than anyone had anticipated, what could that mean for people's emotions?

Impatience? Tension? Annoyance? Resentments?

How does that affect people's thinking?

Really try to imagine yourself in the shoes of the people involved. When they entered negotiations, they probably expected everything to go smoothly.

Perhaps now they feel like they're *losing control*. They feel *uncertainty* about how things will turn out. *What emotion does that trigger? Anxiety? Stress? What emotion would it trigger for you if you were in their shoes?*

Understanding this, *How would that change your approach?*

Another question to ask yourself in such situation is, *What Would The Ideal Emotional State Be?* For everyone involved, including myself.

How Can I Create An Environment To Enable This Emotional State?

While you're thinking through these questions, you might also take a look at the bigger picture by asking yourself:

How Do I Want All Of The Parties To Feel Once The Negotiations Have Finished?

What are the range of outcomes that would leave everyone feeling like they've won?

What are the range of outcomes that would leave one side feeling victorious while the other side feels bitter?

IF I COULD REVERSE ANY 3 DECISIONS, THEN WHAT?

Intelligent people make stupid decisions all of the time.

An interesting example of this is Long Term Capital Management, a hedge fund that was filled with some of the world's smartest people including Nobel Prize winners. And yet, their hedge fund ended in disaster with their failed trades, after having loaded up on *enormous* leverage, nearly brought the entire financial system down with them.

An interesting question to reflect on is, *If I Could Reverse Any 3 Financial Decisions, Then How Much Money Would I Have?*

This can help you better understand your decision making track record and where your blind spots are.

You can use this question on different areas of your life:

- If I Could Reverse Any 3 **Career** Decisions, Then What Would Happen?
-If I Could Reverse Any 3 **Health** Decisions, Then How Would I Be?
-If I Could Reverse Any 3 **Relationship** Decisions, Then How

Would My Relationships Look Like Today?

Reflect on the question and see whether there are any patterns.

WHAT'S THE DOWNSIDE?

It's useful to develop the habit of asking this question before making a decision — especially any major decisions.

This will help you avoid making any potentially bad choices that you'll come to regret. The choice would be even worse if the upside was small but the potential downside big.

Ask yourself, *What's the Downside?*

If there are any major downsides, consider the probability of the downside and whether it's an acceptable risk for you.

Let's say for example that you're thinking about investing in a business.

The upside in your view is that you can 30x your money. The downside is that you lose your entire investment. You assess the probability of the downside to be 20%.

The odds are in your favor and you decide that the upside makes the risk worth it.

Now let's say that the minimum investment required is $100,000 and that represents *all of your life* savings.

This obviously changes the dynamic significantly and the next question to consider is whether losing your life savings is an acceptable risk. In such a case, you may take into consideration your risk profile, your disposable income, your age, and so on.

For many people, it's probably no longer an acceptable risk, despite the potentially huge payoff, simply because the risk of *total loss* is unacceptable. There's the further risk that your assessment of the downside risk was optimistic because you *want* to believe that it will work out well. Generally speaking, being able to stay in the game means avoid getting wiped out or taking potentially large losses. Hence the investment maxim that if you protect the downside, the upside will take care of itself.

Once you're clear on the downside risks and decide to proceed after careful consideration, then you can actively take steps to mitigate any risks you've identified thus far.

For example, before I started publishing books, I made a list of the potential downsides. One of the major ones is losing my Amazon publishing account where I publish my books and get paid. I went through Reddit and found hundreds of posts from anxious writers who got their accounts suspended or banned — sometimes only one month after getting published! I made a list of some of the most common reasons that got them into trouble and put those on my "not to do" list. Some of the reasons were pretty obvious while others not so much.

Of course this doesn't guarantee that nothing will happen to my publishing account but it lowers the overall risk of getting suspended or banned.

When making a decision, ask yourself, *What's the Downside?*

IS THERE ASYMMETRY HERE?

Take a moment to determine whether there's an asymmetric cost-benefit dynamic at play.

There's asymmetry if the **benefit far outweighs the costs**, which is great, or if the **cost far outweighs the benefits**, which is not so great.

The typical example used to demonstrate the idea of asymmetric payoff is investing. If you invest $50 in the stock of XYZ company, your total downside is limited to that $50 (this is the maximum amount of money that you can lose) while your upside is theoretically unlimited.

An essential component of figuring out asymmetry is judging what the odds are.

For example, let's say you're thinking about commercial flights. The benefit is that you get to your desired location much faster than any alternative modes of transport. The cost is that the plane can potentially crash causing fatalities. Scary stuff, right? You might think that there's asymmetry here because the potential cost is so great.

However, the odds of the downside is so small (around 1

in 11 million plane crashes compared to 1 in 5,000 for car crashes) that it's really quite negligible. This is why insurers feel comfortable insuring commercial pilots that *fly all the time*.

Thinking about asymmetry is not very intuitive but it forces us to think about probabilities of both the upside as well as the downside, as well as how much we really value something.

To get you thinking about this, ask yourself what the potential benefits and costs are of the following activities:

- Going on a first date
- Striking a conversation with a stranger
- Going to a networking event
- Reading a book
- Changing things up (country, routine, diet, and so on)
- Sharing your work publicly

What are other activities that have positive asymmetric payoffs and that interests you? What are activities that have negative asymmetric payoffs?

Ultimately, the goal is to consciously favor activities that have huge upsides yet limited downside, and to avoid activities that have huge downside risks but limited benefits.

HOW DO I INVERT THIS?

Man muss immer umkehren (Invert, Always Invert) — Carl Jacobi

When you're trying to solve an issue, ask yourself, *How Do I Invert This?*

Carl Jacobi, a German mathematician, solved difficult problems by addressing it backwards. By studying the opposite and thinking through the problem or question in reverse.

While Einstein's colleagues were all trying to revise James Maxwell's electromagnetic theory to be consistent with Newton's laws, Einstein reversed course and revised Newton's law instead.

Karl Popper, the famous Austrian-British philosopher, is known for his falsification idea which states that science doesn't advance by proving theories true; instead it advances by proving theories *false*. The belief in Europe that all swans are white was disproved by the sighting black swans in Australia. No matter how many white swans we find, we cannot prove that all swans are white. However, by finding one single black swan, we can disprove the theory.

Consider how you can apply inversion to different areas of your life.

Here are a few examples:

How do I increase my earnings? becomes *How do I protect my earnings?*
How do I increase my investment returns? becomes *How do I avoid losing money?*
How do I become healthy? becomes *How do I avoid becoming sick?*
How do I become a good father? becomes *How do I avoid becoming a bad father?*
How do I make a good decision? becomes *How do I avoid making bad decision?*

It's often helpful to brainstorm a list of what the inverse scenario would look like.

For example, *How can I fail at becoming a good father? How can I fail in my relationships? How can I fail at setting up my business?*

When I was starting my Amazon FBA business and was thinking about how things might go wrong, I did some research on Reddit and various eCommerce forums. There were a lot of panicked posts from people that had their Amazon seller accounts shut down by Amazon for a variety of reasons. I made a list of the reasons that got those sellers banned from selling on Amazon to hopefully avoid the same thing happening to me.

There are times when it's not obvious what the inverse might look like and it's worth taking the time to do some research. For example, to avoid losing money in an investment, one thing I can do is avoid investing in any companies that are fraudulent and run by cons. But then again, how do I know which companies are actually fraudulent? After all, Bernie Madoff, Elizabeth Holmes, and Sam Bankman-Fried have all conned very high profile investors.

One thing I can do is study well-known cons and fraudulent operators, the behaviours that such con artists often exhibit, and consider red flags I should be looking for. While this doesn't guarantee that I'll avoid fraudulent companies, I'll at least be alert for signs that I would consider to be red flags, and let new relevant knowledge and experience update my understanding along the way.

I can also research the mistakes of other well-known investors to better understand what to avoid by reading their investment letters and books. For example, one such book is *What I Learned Losing a Million Dollars* by Jim Paul where he talks about the importance of investor emotion and psychology:

I didn't lose that kind of money simply because of a faulty analysis... [I]t was the psychological distortion accompanying a series of successes, drawing my ego into the market position and setting me up for the disastrous loss.

All too often a meteoric rise triggers a precipitous fall. Personalizing success sets people up for disastrous failure.

Learning how not to lose money is more important than learning how to make money.

As you think through your decisions, let it become a habit to think through things forwards and backwards.

Ask yourself, *How Do I Invert This?*

WHAT AM I MISSING?

The riskiest moment is when you think you're right. — Peter Bernstein

Before making any major decisions, ask yourself, *What Am I Missing?*

Did I check my assumptions?

Did I get counter perspectives?

What am I avoiding?

Did I get all of the relevant facts?

How else can I be thinking about this?

WHAT ARE THE CONTROLLABLES HERE?

Of all existing things some are in our power, and others are not in our power.

In our power are thought, impulse, will to get and will to avoid, and, in a word, everything which is our own doing.

Things not in our power include the body, property, reputation, office, and, in a word, everything which is not our own doing.

It's worth knowing in each situation what the controllable factors are. — Epictetus

What exactly is within your control? What is actually knowable?

Within the world of investing, this is a question which Buffett and Munger constantly assess. Anything that's not controllable or knowable is a waste of time and energy to think about. It goes into a dedicated basked called the "too hard pile".

That includes things like trying to predict what the economy is going to do, despite the fact that many pundits do it. It also includes companies that are too hard to evaluate or understand.

In each situation you're considering, identify what the controllable factors are. There's no point thinking or worrying about things that fall outside of your control. If it's not knowable, it doesn't really matter since there's not much you can do about it anyway.

You know with certainty that you can workout at the gym and that can alter your state of mind. That's within your control. You don't know when you'll die. That's outside of your control (for now, at least!).

You can't control how many sales you'll make but you can control how awesome your product is.

Ask Yourself, *What Are The Controllables Here?*

HOW DO I KNOW WHAT I KNOW?

It's good to question our knowledge occasionally.

Afterall, how can we be certain that what we believe to be true isn't completely wrong?

Our worldview is shaped by many factors and those influences often lie beneath the surface, outside of conscious thought.

A friend says something to you, then it comes up again in an article that you read or in your Facebook Newsfeed, then the next day you see something about it on Twitter. At some stage without realizing it, you've started to form an opinion about what's true.

You've adopted a belief without carefully considering it first.

If we don't actively apply critical thought to our pre-existing ideas and beliefs, we become more susceptible to false information.

Consider the news that you're currently reading. They are written by journalists. People like you and me that have their own psychological biases and worldviews.

The journalists that are covering this major issues outside of their domain must consult experts to write their stories. That leads one to wonder:

-How do they choose the experts they talk to and how do they filter the information they receive from experts?
-How much do the journalists themselves know about the topic?
-Are they equipped to make this judgement given that they themselves are not an expert in the field?
-How much are they influenced by their own incentives like getting more clicks and views?

Additional Questions

-How do I know this to be true?
-Am I exposed to counterarguments? If not, where can I gather such arguments?
-How does this person know what they know?
-Do I assume this person is an expert because they have general intelligence?
-Is the fact that they talk very confidently and with certainty about how the future unfold influence my own beliefs?

HOW CLOSE AM I TO THIS?

The closer you are to something, the more your judgment can be impaired.

I have an engineering friend that's extremely intelligent and highly capable but works at a terrible organization. She has been there for over 8 years and it's obvious to everyone around her that she should take her talents elsewhere. But it's not clear to her and probably feels very uncomfortable to her to change things up.

When we see these kind of things happening to others, it's usually easy and clear to see. However, when it's happening to us, the picture starts to blur quite quickly.

When you're in the heat of the moment, it helps to remember this and consider that, *Hey, maybe this is a good time to have some distance*?

The question *How Close Am I To This?* is especially useful to ask in situations where you need to make important decisions.

To consider the question of how close you are to something, consider whether any of the following factors are present:

Emotion — whether emotions are charged, as they tend to get in relationships and business.

Repetition — repetition in activities, repeating something many times, repeating the same patterns of thoughts, hearing the same things over and over again, through time.

Vested Interest — when you have a stake. For example, once you start working for someone, you start your own company, you have equity in a company.

Of course, these can and do overlap, and that combination will typically magnify the overall effect.

Emotions

The stronger the feeling, the stronger the impairment to judgement.

For example, if you develop very strong emotions about someone you're dating, you're probably not going to see that person's traits very clearly, at least not initially. Everything will be rainbows and butterflies. When they do something that seems off, it gets swiftly swept under a rug. Or your mind will write a story that fits their behavior according to your narrative. In other words, what you usually might consider to be a red flag will barely flash as a blip on your radar.

It doesn't just happen in relationships. It can happen in any sphere of life including in the business arena. Bob Iger

(Chairman of Disney) talks about the disastrous years of Michael Ovitz as President of Disney in his book, *The Ride of a Lifetime*, and how being emotionally attached to an outcome led to some bad and very costly years at Disney.

Bob writes in his memoir, *When you find yourself in moments of hoping something will work, without knowing how it will work, that should ring alarm bells.*

Whether it's relationships, business or something else, you'll sometimes get that subtle feeling that something's off. Don't override that feeling, especially if it's a nagging one.

Let it surface and explore it.

Repetition

The harder you work, the more confidence you get. But you may be working hard on something that is false. — Charlie Munger

We have a tendency to develop tunnel vision the more we do something.

This is because the more we do something, the more we reinforce the idea in our head that this is the way to do it.

Do you know those situations when an outsider comes in and says, *Hey, why didn't you just try doing X to solve this issue?* Then you think, *Oh, of course! It's so obvious. Why didn't I think of it?*

It's because they're free of the preconceptions about how things should be done and they have distance to the situation so they can see with more clarity.

Consider that there was very little progress in our understanding of cancer for decades with established beliefs in the research community about how cancer progressed. The National Cancer Institute then decided to recruit people from *outside* the health profession, like physicists (!), which ultimately helped provide new insights and breakthroughs by simply asking better questions about how cancer develops.

Vested Interest

I noticed an interesting switch that happened a while back when I did consulting. While I was in the process of putting together a proposal for a potential client, I had a ton of ideas about how they can improve their business. I was very confident about all of my ideas and tactics, and I was sure that it was going to make the client a lot of money.

After the proposal got accepted, doubt started to seep into my mind. *Will this even work? How can I be sure?*

Before the engagement started, there was no relationship. I had distance. I was detached.

After it got accepted, I wasn't so sure about it. I noticed a slight block in my ability to be creative and think freely.

I ended up writing a detailed list of top ideas and what to do in each case if things don't work out as planned. *Did I try X? Did I miss Y? Did I make sure to give it an appropriate amount of time to get results?*

Another example is investing in shares. After you purchase shares, your emotional relationship to the shares change.

If they go up, you congratulate yourself on being so smart.

If they go down, you panic and want to sell.

That's why *before* buying shares, it's useful to imagine what can happen and decide what to do in various scenarios.

If the shares double, I will do X.
If the shares halve, I will do Y.
If the shares do nothing, I will do Z.

WHAT ARE THE INCENTIVES?

Show me the incentive and I will show you the outcome. — Charlie Munger

Generally when incentives such as money gets involved, people's ability to see things clearly can become blurred.

Incentives can distort our ability to see the reality.

Sometimes we *want* to see things a certain way if we're motivated enough.

Incentives can be powerful.

Keep this in mind when observing your own behavior or that of others.

When looking at people's behavior, ask yourself, *What Are The Incentives Here?*

WHAT'S THE PATH OF HARDSHIP HERE?

Difficulties strengthen the mind, as labor does the body. — Seneca

Adversity is a crossroads that makes a person choose one of two paths: character or compromise. Every time he chooses character, he becomes stronger, even if that choice brings negative consequences. — John C. Maxwell

We naturally like to do what's easy. To take the path of least resistance. Modern life has become all about taking shortcuts and instant gratification. A magic pill instead of adopting a healthy diet and lifestyle, wanting to get rich quick without doing any actual work, trying to look smart without doing any study.

The only issue is that growth happens when we struggle. Not when we take it easy. By putting in the actual work, you'll already be miles ahead of most people.

Actively seek the challenging path.

It starts with the seemingly small things. Given the choice of going to the gym tonight or chilling with Netflix and wine, the latter option feels more tempting. The same goes for ordering fast food compared to making something healthy.

Spending an hour on social media as opposed to learning something new. Taking the elevator versus walking up the stairs. Saving versus spending. Bringing up a tough conversation versus avoiding the matter altogether.

Avoid letting the mind default to the easy option without any consideration. Other times, it will choose the easy option and rationalize it convincingly. *It's too cold outside to go to the gym. I'll go tomorrow when the weather is better.*

The path of hardship sometimes is precisely the thing that we need to do.

The more you want to avoid something, the more closely you need to take a look at it.

Ask yourself, *What's The Path of Hardship Here?*

HOW CAN I LEARN FROM MY DECISIONS OVER TIME?

Look for **Strengths** and **Weaknesses.**

Over time, I can recognize where my decision making strength and decision making weakness lay by looking over past decisions and their outcomes. Do this as if you're reviewing someone else's scorecard to be more objective.

Look for **Patterns.**

I can see that I make better decisions generally when I'm more detached, less judgmental and feeling calm and relaxed. If I'm very stressed, I'm more likely to make rash decisions. If I'm a little stressed, that's okay and sometimes even beneficial.

Look for **Principles.**

As you look at your decisions over time, you'll see the reasons for your choices emerge. That will make it easier to make future decisions because you can then say, *Ah yes, I've encountered this one before and I know what I need to do.*

Look for Biases.

When I look over my decisions after a period of time has passed, I can see my biases somewhat more clearly. For example, I have a tendency to reach a quick conclusion before getting all of the relevant facts. An extension of that is relying too much on what's easily accessible to me (availability heuristic) and giving too much importance to what's easily available to me instead of looking for disconfirming evidence.

Once you gather your lessons, consider how you can apply them with the question, *What Systems Can I Set Up To Minimize Poor Decision Making?*

MINDFULNESS

The happiness of your life depends upon the quality of your thoughts — Marcus Aurelius

WHY DO I HAVE THIS THOUGHT?

Whatever thoughts, or concepts, or obscuring, or disturbing passions arise are neither to be abandoned nor allowed to control one: they are to be allowed to arise without one's trying to direct or shape them. If one do no more than merely to recognize them as soon as they arise, and persist in so doing, they will come to be realized or to dawn in their true or void form through not being abandoned. — Patanjali

The best meditation is being genuinely curious about the contents of your own mind. — Naval Ravikant

Observe your every thought without judgment.

Take a day for monitoring your thoughts.

Where each and every hour, you ask yourself, *Why Do I Have This Thought?*

Write these down in a journal.

DOES THIS THOUGHT DESERVE TO BE HERE?

Yoga is the control of the ideas in the mind. — Patanjali

All that we are is the result of what we have thought: it is founded on our thoughts, it is made up of our thoughts. If a man speaks or acts with a pure thought, happiness follows him like a shadow that never leaves him. — Gautama Buddha

Therefore the vigorous working of your imagination, which is always so active... must as often be suppressed. Unless you suppress it, it will suppress you. — Anonymous

Your attention is limited. What you give your attention to is what you give your energy, your life force to.

Any thought that's hanging around in your head needs to deserve to be there.

Spend a bit of time thinking about what you would like to think about.

Don't rush to act. Action drives out thought.

When you rush to use your phone first thing in the morning, your thoughts will become dictated by the stimulus you get from social media. It will impact your thinking and set the tone for the rest of your day.

In a hyper connected world where smartphones play a starring role in our lives and influence the thoughts that occupy our minds, it's become even more important to keep our mind protected from unnecessary stimulus.

1. Develop Habit To Monitor Thoughts

The first step is to start becoming aware of the internal dialogue.

It doesn't really matter whether it's a desired thought or not. Don't exercise any judgement. Just make a point of checking in so that you can start to develop the habit of simply monitoring the thoughts that are going on throughout the day. You can start with checking in a few times a day and eventually 10 or 20 times a day.

I like to keep a notebook handy and will just jot down a word or two if I'm in the middle of something like *worried* or *powerful.* If I have more time, then I'll elaborate or even go on to full stream of consciousness writing which I find therapeutic when I need to get something out. Doing this will allow you to become much more self aware and observe some interesting things that happen.

When you're hanging out with friends, checking social media, reading your emails, eating, and going about your daily routine, how often do you pay attention to the thoughts in your mind?

To be the passive observer that says, *Huh, that's interesting,* while you're conscious mind is chattering away.

2. Question The Thought

Once you develop the habit of regularly checking in on your thoughts, you're then able to start building up your mental muscle, kind of like building a fortress around your mind.

You'll no longer allow Facebook, Instagram, Twitter, TikTok or other external stimulus to be the primary driver of your thought. You'll become more assertive in determining what actually occupies your mental real estate.

You can build on top of the thought checking habit by using the question, *Does This Thought Deserve To Be Here?*

Your internal dialogue carries a lot weight. In Step 1, you've learned to paid attention to the conversation that's going on inside your head.

Now you're going to gauge whether the thought deserves to occupy your mind. To see if it's worthy of your attention and mental firepower.

If you decide the thought deserves to be there, then it stays.

If it doesn't, then it's time to get rid of the thought.

3. Replace The Unworthy Thought

I've found it useful to have a few different methods for replacing the unwanted thought ready.

The following are a few options to get you started and give you some ideas for what you'd like to think about when you want something else to be thinking about.

Great Thinkers

Depending on my mood, I'll think on the words of wisdom from great thinkers either by reflecting through memory or reading select passages. The ones that I often think about are Cicero, Plato, Seneca, Epictetus, Marcus Aurelius, and Charlie Munger.

Power Questions

When I have some uninterrupted time available then I'll answer a power question by thinking deeply about it and then writing my thoughts on it in a journal.

Depending on what the actual thought is, it can range from *How Does This Help Me?* to *How Can I Make This An Empowering Story?*

Music

Sometimes you don't need to think about anything.

There are other times when my intuition might say to listen to classical music and appreciate its beauty.

Other times, it's just to be still and meditate.

DOES THIS ENERGIZE ME?

As you go about your day to day activities, ask yourself, *Does This Energize Me?*

Or Does It Take Energy Away From Me?

Be aware of how different thoughts and activities impact your energy levels.

Then take note of them.

Spend a day logging what subtracts energy for you and what gives you energy.

When I'm with X person, I feel more energy.

When I'm reading Y email, I feel less energy.

When I'm thinking Z thought, I feel more energy.

When I'm walking in the park, I feel more energy.

WHAT'S THE PURPOSE HERE?

Be intentional.

For example, going to meetings without an agenda can be a waste of time.

If you have a clear idea of what you need to solve or what question you're trying to answer before going into a meeting, you'll get much more out of it. Be intentional about it.

Before going into a meeting, ask yourself, *What's The Purpose Here?* Be clear about it and write it down.

If the purpose is to brainstorm and generate new ideas, then that's fine. That's the purpose. But if you went in to figure out why your company's customer service levels is deteriorating and you instead end up with a bunch of new product ideas and discuss other random topics, the meeting hasn't achieved what you needed and you need to call yet another meeting.

The same goes for jumping on calls. *What's The Purpose Here?*

Here are some possible answers:

-It's to get the person I'm cold calling to get comfortable with me

and set up a demo.
-It's to answer any objections.
-It's to make the customer feel valued and listened to.
-It's to close the deal.
-It's to get feedback.
-It's to provide feedback.

Another example is for reading books. *What's The Purpose Here?* I want to learn techniques for improving my conversational skills, for example. You'll be much more intentional in searching for answers while you're reading and you'll skim the parts that aren't as important for you.

Sometimes, I've found that I'm reading for the sake of just increasing the number of books I've read instead of aiming for true understanding which is my real purpose.

You're working out. *What's The Purpose Here?* I want to improve my overall health and feel more energy for the day.

When doing an activity, be intentional and ask yourself, *What's The Purpose Here?*

The clearer you are on knowing why you're doing something, the more likely you'll be in achieving it. You'll also know what the expected outcome is and whether what you're doing is actually working.

If the intended result of working out was to get more energy for the day and you just feel tired all of the time, you can try something different in an effort to get the result you're looking for.

AM I PREPARED FOR THIS?

Success breeds complacency. Complacency breeds failure. Only the paranoid survive. — Andy Grove

If an evil has been pondered beforehand, the blow is gentle when it comes. To the fool, however, and to him who trusts in fortune, each event as it arrives 'comes in a new and sudden form,' and a large part of evil, to the inexperienced, consists in its novelty. This is proved by the fact that men endure with greater courage, when they have once become accustomed to them, the things which they had at first regarded as hardships. — Seneca

In your lifetime, you'll deal with all kinds of losses and setbacks.

The death of loved ones, pandemics, natural disasters, economic crashes, wars, health problems, divorces/break ups, major business/career problems.

The occurrence of these things will fall largely outside of your control and certainly can feel devastating when it strikes out of the blue.

Premeditatio Malorum

Instead of letting the events land a heavy blow, you can choose to take away some of that power by anticipating such things in advance and prepare for the storm that you know is inevitable. Tragedies are an inseparable part of our condition. You may as well learn to get comfortable with that reality. Your relationship with unavoidable setbacks is within your control as is your ability to prepare.

This premeditation of the coming storm is what Stoics refer to in Latin as *premeditatio malorum*.

For example, the cyclical nature of the economy means that there will be booms and busts. With that bit of knowledge, you can put aside extra personal/business savings during the good times to cushion you in the bad times. While this sounds simple in principle, how often is this actually done in practice?

The reason we don't prepare is because we expect the good times to last forever. And then we're caught off guard when there's a crash. We think we'll be able to take a flight anytime to a holiday destination we like until there's a pandemic. We think we'll live long into some unimaginable distant future until we're suddenly old and frail. We think our family will be around forever until they're suddenly taken away.

We have a psychological tendency to extrapolate our most recent experience far into the future. The subconscious is thinking to itself, *How things are right now is how things will be indefinitely.*

Since this feeling happens beneath the surface, we don't realize this thought consciously. And yet that's the basis with which we operate from. And exactly the reason why it can be dangerous. It lulls us into a false sense of safety and security.

If business is good now, you'll think business will be good indefinitely with little regard for your competition and the shifting market. The bigger the success, the more exaggerated this sense of complacency.

Choose to be prepared. Ask yourself the question, *Am I Prepared? What Can I Do To Prepare?*

Mental Acceptance

Sometimes it will be a case of mentally accepting the inevitable. The things that fall outside of our control. People die. People get fired. People get stabbed. People break up. Natural disasters happen. Pandemics happen. Businesses get shut down. Wars happen. In short, shit happens.

One way to mentally prepare for such case is by thinking, *If X happens, then I will do Y.*

If I'm forced to stay indoors, then I'll tell myself that it's a great opportunity to catch up on the books that I've been meaning to read and reconnect with friends that I've lost touch with.
If my restaurant goes bankrupt, then I'll tell myself that the worst case scenario is that I'll start looking for a job.
If my husband divorces me, then I'll tell myself that it's for the best and stay with my friend Margaret while focusing on

the controllables like journaling, exercising, hanging out with friends.

If my health fails me, then I'll express my love to friends and family, feel gratitude for the time spent on this earth with my loved ones and I'll depart with grace.

If you spend a bit of time meditating through these scenarios, it helps to soften the blow when it comes.

Preparing for the Storm

Other times, there are actions you can take in advance to make it easier to deal with the storm or prevent it altogether.

It is useful to create a detailed list of the things that can go wrong and the accompanying steps you can take.

Premeditate the storm and ask yourself, *What Can I Do To Prepare for X?*

The business needs a buffer for difficult times. What specific actions can I take? I can put aside 3% of all sales away so that I don't even see the money and have it saved up for a rainy day.

My wife may leave me one day. What can I do to prepare? I can become more attentive to her, start reading relationship books, suggest seeing a therapist together to build a stronger relationship, and take it from there.

I may lose my job one day. *What can I do to prepare?* I can ensure build a buffer to ensure that I have sufficient savings while I search for another job. I can ensure that I'm performing to the best of my abilities at work, going above and beyond with dedication, maintaining good relationships with my colleagues and constantly getting honest feedback from which I can learn.

Think through the possible storms and you will handle hardships that come your way with grace.

Ask yourself the question, *Am I Prepared? What Can I Do To Prepare for X?*

IS IT CONTROLLABLE?

We spend a lot of time thinking and worrying about things that lie outside of our control.

Before you start thinking about these things, ask yourself, *Is It Controllable?*

One example is spending an inordinate amount of time thinking about whether someone likes you. That's largely outside of your control. How that person feels is entirely up to them. You can obviously change your own behaviour which can influence the relationship but ultimately the thoughts of another person is outside your realm of control.

Other examples include whether stock prices move favorably, what the weather will be tomorrow, and so on.

Instead, choose to focus things that are actually within your control. There are so many things that are within your control it makes very little sense to dwell on the things that are not, even more so if those things upset you.

You can choose the thoughts that occupy your mind. You can control what you eat. Who you hang out with. How well you treat the people around you. What you read. How you spend your free time. How often you exercise. How you react.

The next time you start dwelling on something, ask yourself, *Is It Controllable?*

If it's not, let it go or use the worry as a trigger to do something positive with it.

A related question to consider: *Is It Knowable?*

For example, we can know our own thoughts and feelings.

But we can only *guess* as to the inner world of other people, what they really think or feel about us.

IS THIS REALLY NECESSARY?

There are many benefits to keeping it simple.

You get more time.

You're able to do the fewer things you're doing better.

You're more focused and less distracted.

Consider the 80/20 rule.

20 percent of your activities are responsible for 80 percent of your results.

In other words, only a few of the things you do actually matter, **but those few things matter a lot.**

Before jumping to act, ask yourself, *Is This Really Necessary?*

Remove any unnecessary thoughts and unnecessary actions.

PERSPECTIVE

The essence of the independent mind lies not in what it thinks, but in how it thinks. — Christopher Hitchens

DOES IT WORK?

Insanity is doing the same thing over and over and expecting different results. — Albert Einstein

A simple question.

Yet one we forget to ask when we get unexpected results.

Why?

Because sometimes reality doesn't conform to our beliefs. Because sometimes we just really want something to work, despite evidence to the contrary. Maybe we're committed to a particular way of doing things. Maybe charged emotions make it difficult to see things as they are.

So we decide to ignore reality instead.

It can be the way we're communicating that's leading to conflict. The weight loss program that seems to be making things worse. The advertising campaign that seems to be burning money.

The first step is to acknowledge reality by asking, *Does It Work?*

Only then can we take the next step to assess, learn and then figure out what we can do differently.

AM I ENTITLED TO HAVE AN OPINION ON THIS?

Socrates use to go around saying that, "I know nothing except the fact of my own ignorance."

He would then question the wise men of Athens, learning what they knew from first principles. Through his pointed questioning method, he would pop his adversary's bubble and expose inconsistencies in their beliefs and ideas.

There's wisdom in knowing when to have an opinion and, perhaps more importantly, when *not* to have one.

Opinions are casually thrown about everywhere these days.

Everyone has something to say on a number of topics. It might even feel like we need to have an opinion on everything. Maybe it looks intelligent to have an opinion on everything. Or it just looks stupid to not have an opinion on certain things and we feel a need to form an opinion to fit in.

Either way, it's smarter to know where the boundaries of our knowledge is than pretending to have it much bigger than it is in reality and saying things without actual knowledge on the subject.

We don't need to have an opinion on *anything.*

The more we voice our opinion on something out loud, the more we're hammering that idea into our brain. Do this enough times and we run the risk of becoming attached to a belief, even if it's false, when it's said enough times.

It then becomes very difficult to let go of that belief, even when strong contradictory evidence has appeared.

It's good practice to ask yourself before forming an opinion, *Am I Entitled To Have An Opinion On This?*

Following from the Socrates method, you can use this prompt to start a line of questioning so that you can come to thoroughly understand the different positions including those that have opposing opinions.

Jamie Dimon, the CEO of Chase, once commented during an interview, *Read the other side. Some of your fellow citizens have good reasons to believe something different than you do. I try to think sometimes about where are they right? Not are they wrong. You'll become a better thinker. And you earn peoples' respect.*

You can also use this practice to question any existing opinions you already hold.

Stanford professor Paul Saffo uses a framework *Strong Opinions, Weakly Held.* Here's how he describes it.

Allow your intuition to guide you to a conclusion, no matter how imperfect — this is the 'strong opinion' part. Then — and this is the 'weakly held' part — prove yourself wrong.

Engage in creative doubt. Look for information that doesn't fit, or indicators that point in an entirely different direction. Eventually your intuition will kick in and a new hypothesis will emerge out of the rubble, ready to be ruthlessly torn apart once again.

WILL MY IDEA CHANGE IN 10 YEARS?

Any year that passes in which you don't destroy one of your best loved ideas is a wasted year — Charlie Munger

Think about how we form ideas and opinions. How many of them go through critical thinking and gets stress tested? The odds are, not many.

The more we talk or write about our ideas and opinions, the more they get cemented in our brain, even if they're false. The effect is amplified if we're publishing papers and building a career around those ideas.

That's the reasoning behind the saying, *science progresses one funeral at a time*. It's difficult, even for brilliant physicists, to change their mind when the facts have changed because they've built their success on those very ideas.

Imagine spending 20 years of your academic life publishing papers, giving lectures, writing books to the wide acclaim of friends and colleagues. Suddenly a young hotshot that happens to be the same student you lectured to upends all of your life's work with a brilliant insight.

What's your reaction going to be? As much we'd like to think otherwise, you're probably not going to embrace the hotshot and say, *Oh yes, I was wrong, kiddo. Great stuff. I'm now going to change my mind on this.* You'll more likely stick to your guns until the very end. And that's what typically ends up happening in the real world.

The young rising star on the other hand has no specific love or attachment to the established ideas. The ambitious student looking to make a mark on the world will gladly kill off any of the ideas that are currently in vogue and will be more open to disconfirming evidence. It's easier to look at reality accurately when your vision isn't blurred by preconceptions about how things are or should be. Until of course that rising star gets attached to ideas the same way the old guard did and replaces the establishment. And so the cycle continues and science waits until a new generation comes along to dispel old ideas.

Stress Testing Your Ideas and Opinions

Time Test

It takes a lot of conscious effort to kill your beloved ideas and opinions. It can be even painful and emotional at times.

To make it slightly easier, consider the ideas and opinions that you hold dear. Then ask yourself, *how true will they remain in 10 years? Will it change at all in 10 years? Will it change in 100 years?*

Putting a bigger time horizon helps to create a bit of distance and gives you some space to detach.

Try to imagine events unfolding through time. Fast forward to the future and then rewind back to the present.

Do this exercise a number of times to loosen the attachment to tightly held ideas.

Disconfirming Evidence Habit

Charles Darwin trained himself from early on to consciously consider any disconfirming evidence that would contradict his hypothesis. This is arguably the main reason for his remarkable discoveries.

You can learn from Darwin by building a habit of actively seeking disconfirming evidence so that you have opportunities to stress test your ideas and opinions.

Whenever we come across evidence to the contrary, the natural tendency is to ignore or dismiss it. We're far more receptive to evidence which confirms our existing beliefs.

That's why you need to proactively look for evidence that doesn't fit your narrative to overcome your natural bias against such evidence.

WHAT ARE MY BLIND SPOTS?

It's easy to spot other people's psychological blind spots.

It's very difficult to detect it in ourself.

To help you find your blind spots:

- Think about inconsistencies between what most people say about you and what you believe about yourself. What are the main differences?

- Think about the times where most of your decisions have not worked out. Are there similarities?

WHAT'S SURPRISING?

We often look for evidence to confirm what we already believe.

Let's say you believe that a particular brand is bad. Then when you're scrolling on social media, you notice some bad press about them. You remember it and pay attention to it. You might even mention it to friends the next time you see them. *Did you hear what happened to these guys? I told ya. They're baaaad news.*

But then, some months later when you see that they've won an award on your newsfeed, you scroll by without it registering at all and you move on to the next item.

This is very natural. We all do it.

We tend to hangout with people who share our world views.

It makes us comfortable.

But if we're interested in learning what's true, what's real, we need to pay attention to *all evidence* and be open-minded about it.

I've found that by flipping this around and asking, *What's Surprising?* it's much easier to get my mind to focus on information that I would otherwise ignore. And best of all, it's done in a non-threatening way that doesn't damage my ego.

This question allows us to consciously shift from seeking confirming evidence (which we already do *unconsciously*) to seeking disconfirming evidence (which we can try to do *consciously*).

You might even find joy in this process and use it as an opportunity for learning.

Once we find disconfirming evidence, we can then dig deeper.

-Why is this surprising?
-What was my expectation?
-How can I reconcile the differences?

By asking *What's Surprising?*, we're approaching information in an open-minded way with the mindset of a learner.

WHAT AM I AFRAID OF?

You never change your life until you step out of your comfort zone; change begins at the end of your comfort zone — Roy T. Bennett

Learn to get uncomfortable. Sit with the feeling instead of distracting yourself. Ask yourself, *What Am I Afraid Of?*

Dig deep and explore it. *What's the source of your fear?* The deeper the feeling of discomfort, the more there is to discover in the process. Write your unfiltered thoughts down, without judgement or attachment to the thoughts.

Sometimes it's the fear of telling the truth because you might end up hurting someone. Or the fear of getting up on stage and speaking and being exposed as a fraud. Or fear of losing a friend. Or fear of being alone.

One of the greatest discoveries a man makes, one of his great surprises, is to find he can do what he was afraid he couldn't do — Henry Ford

Process the thing that makes you afraid and do the things that scare you the most.

Other angles:

- What Am I Afraid To Know?
- What Do I Sense Without Knowing?
- What's The One Thing I Don't Want To Accept?

Find them by asking yourself, *What Am I Afraid Of?*

WHICH ONE OF THOSE AM I DEALING WITH?

When you find yourself facing a challenging situation, try asking yourself, *Which One Of Those Am I Dealing With?*

Categorizing what you're facing into "another one of those" helps you detach, make sense of things, and see more clearly.

If you become very emotional, you're less likely to think clearly about it and engage your brain in creative problem-solving.

Asking this question will reinforce the idea that you're not the only one dealing with this kind of situation. Imagine all of the people before you that have faced similar issues, and have ultimately found a way to deal with it. Perhaps someone on this planet is facing the same situation at this very moment.

Take comfort in knowing that this is not a unique situation in which you alone are facing.

Once you start seeing that, it'll become easier to distance yourself from the challenge at hand, reduce any potential anxiety or tension arising from what's happening, and start working on what needs to happen next.

RUI ZHI DONG

IS IT SIGNAL OR NOISE?

When processing new information, consider for a moment whether it's signal or noise.

In order to capture your attention, a lot of items you'll see on social media or in the newspapers are designed to look like it's **important and newsworthy.**

Most news items are designed to get an emotional response.

Getting your attention is valuable.

Everything is pitched as **breaking news** when most of it is just noise, and sometimes downright toxic.

A general rule of thumb is that short-term information more often than not is noise. Focus on the longer term trends.

How your weight fluctuates on a day to day basis is not as important as how your weight moves over a larger time span.

How your investment's share price is doing minute to minute matters less than they change year to year and how the business itself is actually doing — are they delighting their customers or clients every day?

Recognize noise for what it is and don't get distracted by it.

In 2009, a Stanford business professor split her class into groups and gave a challenge. Each group would get $5 and had a two-hour window to make as much money as possible. Each group would need to present what they did at the end to the class.

Most groups predictably focused on the $5 and how to leverage the cash to make the most possible. For example, they used the money to buy and sell items, making a small profit.

The most successful group ignored the $5 altogether, recognizing a more valuable resource: their presentation time to a room full of Stanford students.

They pitched this time slot to companies eager to recruit from Stanford and sold their presentation space for a whopping $650. They ignored the money as noise in this case and used creative thinking to produce results.

Try to zoom out and ask yourself what the **big picture** is.

We have a natural tendency to overweight the short-term and underweight the long-term. That's why we tend to overestimate what we can achieve in a year and underestimate what we can achieve in ten years.

It can be sometimes difficult to assess whether a signal is actually a signal.

In his book, *Only The Paranoid Survive*, Andrew Grove, the former CEO of Intel, shares his methodology for thinking about the whether a fundamental strategic shift is taking place:

Think about the change in your environment, technological or otherwise, as a blip on your radar screen. You can't tell what that blip represents at first, but you keep watching radar scan after radar scan, looking to see if the object is approaching, what its speed is, and what shape it takes as it comes closer.

Even if it lingers in your periphery, you still keep an eye on it, because its course and speed may change.

The balance might shift and what we once correctly determined was noise might well emerge as a signal we had better pay heed to.

Despite the fact that Andrew's book was published in the late 1980s, this principle remains revelant to this day. For example, all of the hype a decade ago around artificial intelligence was just noise. But this may indeed be shifting and now a signal. Time will tell.

It's a useful framework to keep in mind of remembering to separate signal from noise.

Ignore the trivial. Focus on the signal.

Ask yourself, *Is It Signal Or Noise?*

WHAT'S THE LOW HANGING FRUIT HERE?

We have a tendency to overcomplicate and miss the simple things. Especially when we're very close to it.

When considering a problem or goal, ask yourself, *What's the Low Hanging Fruit Here?*

If you're not trying to solve a specific problem, keep it very broad:

- *What's the low hanging fruit in my business?*
- *What's the low hanging fruit in my career?*
- *What's the low hanging fruit in my relationship?*
- *What's the low hanging fruit in my finances?*

This way, you can consider about ideas that you wouldn't usually think about.

Avoid missing the obvious things to do. They might seem as clear as day to an outside observer but less so once you become too close to the situation.

For the big issues, spend at least 30 or 40 minutes reflecting on the question and writing down an unfiltered list as the ideas come to you. I find this creative process over a cup of coffee at a nice cafe to be fun and rewarding!

Don't analyze during the brainstorming session.

You can process the list later and choose the ideas that are good. Just keep writing as the thought comes to you.

Sometimes, it will be about just identifying the simple and obvious thing. Gaining perspective on seemingly boring things like doubling down on what's *already working* and excluding everything else to maintain focus.

Other times, it will be new insights. Like taking advantage of things you have but don't use to generate income. You might only use your car during the weekends, for instance, and decide to rent it out during the week. You might be a college student with great course notes on your computer which you later realize that you can sell online. You might be a manufacturing company that's produced waste for years which you suddenly realize can actually be reused as material for an entirely different product line and start a new profitable division.

It can be a simple matter of delegating (hiring a cleaner), automating (using software to automate something you've been doing manually) or eliminating an activity altogether.

Ask yourself, *What's the Low Hanging Fruit Here?*

RELATIONSHIPS

*The love you gave in life keeps people alive
beyond their time* — Cicero

HOW CAN I MAKE MY RELATIONSHIP EVEN MORE BEAUTIFUL?

This is a question to brainstorm on and create a list.

Include everything from seemingly small things to more grandiose items.

Can I change the way I communicate? Can I change the way that I listen? What does a perfect relationship look like to me? How would I behave in the most ideal relationship?

Can I change the way I show my love and appreciation?

Can I change the way I create excitement and passion?

What's a belief that will help my relationship which I will adopt? What's a belief that is not helping my relationship which I need to remove?

Is there anything getting in the way of the relationship being absolutely incredible?

WHY HAVE I INVITED THIS PERSON INTO MY LIFE?

When you're spending a significant amount of time with a person, it's worth asking, *Why Have I Invited This Person Into My Life?*

What is it about that person that attracts you? That draws you?

Think about the qualities. The way you feel. It's also good to remember these things when you're feeling upset or hurt at the same person.

It'll be revealing, not only about the person you're spending time with but also about yourself.

Maybe it's the way they listen to you. It makes you feel heard and they listen with care and love. Maybe they bring out the best in you and make you want to be a better person. Maybe you share a hobby that you can talk about for hours on end.

Listen to your intuition. It doesn't necessarily need to be positive. Don't filter it. Simply write it down and process later.

Ask yourself, *Why Have I Invited This Person Into My Life?*

WHERE'S MY TRIBE?

It's been said that we are the *average of the five people we spend the most time with.*

Don't underestimate the powerful influence the people you hang out with can have on you. If you're surrounded by criminals, there's a higher chance that you'll become a criminal too. If you're surrounded by people that only see the worst in people, your views on people will probably change.

This goes the other way around too. If you're a heavy drinker, there's a higher chance your social circle drinks heavily too. If you're a heavy smoker, there's a higher chance your friends smoke too.

Spend some time to reflect on whether the people you're with are the ones you want in your tribe.

Do they share your aspirations? Do they share your values? Do they share your habits? Are they the kind of people you want to spend most of your time hanging out with? If you can choose any 5 people to be in your tribe, who would they be and why?

Maybe you're surrounded by exactly the people you want in your life. Or perhaps there's an opportunity to add different people into your life.

You can also link your tribe to what you're currently getting into.

For example, if you're getting into running marathons, you can join your local marathon club that meets weekly. If you're looking to start a business, you can join a business mastermind.

Ask yourself, *Where's My Tribe?*

DO I SURROUND MYSELF WITH INSPIRING PEOPLE?

Ask yourself, *Who do I find inspiring?*

Think about the people you hang out with as well as the people you have never met.

What are the things about them that I find inspiring?

If you are not inspired by the people you're surrounded with, ask yourself, *Who specifically would I surround myself with?*

Who are the people that I want to meet the most?

Forget for a moment how you might go about actually meeting them.

Just think about all of the people that you find inspiring and make a list.

Then after you're done brainstorming, write the reasons why you find them inspiring and what you'd like to learn from them.

If you already have thoughts about how you might go about

meeting them, you can add that too.

There's something powerful about writing down your intentions on a piece of paper.

I wrote in my journal in 2016, *It would be really great if I could meet Mark Manson in person.*

Two years later, I met him at an event in the Four Seasons at Punta Mita, Mexico where we shared a beer along with his wife.

I now have an updated list of people that I'd like to meet including Ray Dalio, Charlie Munger, Ed Thorp, among others. These are people who have made a deep impact on my thinking and the way I approach life.

WHY AM I JUDGING?

When you see a good person, think of becoming like her. When you see someone not so good, reflect on your own weak points. — Confucius

We judge ourselves by our intentions and everyone else by their actions. — Stephen Covey

Whenever I find myself judging someone, I try to use that feeling to trigger the question, *Why Am I Judging?*

We human beings have a natural tendency to judge others.

It's comforting, helps us make sense of things, and validates us.

What I've found is that the stronger my reaction (*that person is a bit lazy* versus *that person is completely useless!*), the more there is to learn about myself than the actual person that I'm judging.

As such, I try remind myself to let such moments be a trigger to reflect. A signal to turn inwards.

Sometimes it reveals something that I'm uncomfortable with in myself.

If I feel strongly about someone's laziness for example, then it reveals more about myself — that I myself am lazy and I'm not okay with it and therefore react emotionally when I see it in others.

The signals to look for is emotion and vocabulary.

Someone that has been late to all of the past meetings — you have data points that tell you this person's behavioral trait and you have good reasons to presume that this person will probably continue to be late to future meetings. You can do this without having emotions attached. You're just identifying a person's characteristic.

However, once you start getting angry about it (maybe it feels personal) and use labels, that's when it becomes a sign to turn inward and reflect.

Certainly in cases where being late to meetings is unacceptable, that can be raised and dealt with in the proper manner.

The next time you find yourself judging, considering asking the question, *Why Am I Judging?*

The greater the emotion, the more there is to learn and explore.

WHAT ELSE COULD THIS MEAN?

If you and me were sitting in a cafe, and then suddenly some guy sitting next to us starts yelling at us, what would that mean for you?

Maybe you'd think the guy is crazy. Maybe you'd think there must be something wrong with me. Maybe you'd think that person knows me and is angry at me.

The point is that there's a wide array of possible interpretations. You can have 10 people sitting in a cafe watching the same thing but come away with *10 different interpretations...*

Despite this, we often go with our first conclusion and stick with it.

Someone is late for a meeting. Conclusion: *He doesn't respect my time.*

She's replying slowly to my texts. Conclusion: *She's no longer interested in me.*

I didn't get invited to a work event. Conclusion: *I'm going to get fired.*

When you catch yourself jumping to negative conclusions, ask yourself, *What Else Could This Mean?*

It might feel unnatural at first because our brain isn't used to having its conclusion being questioned, especially when our mind is already made up about what a particular event means.

Just keep asking the question. Over and over again.

Eventually your mind will relent.

It will give you more interpretations and put your original conclusion in doubt.

As you ask this question over time, you'll start seeing patterns between stimulus and the stories they trigger, giving you more insight about how your mind operates.

AM I ATTACHED?

Whenever we get overly attached to a person, a thing, an outcome, an image, an idea — our views become distorted. Our emotions start to override our reasoning. We become blind to reality and we only see what we want to see.

That can lead to terrible decision making.

To avoid such an outcome, ask yourself, *Am I Attached? Is this affecting my ability to see the reality of things?*

Be honest with yourself. It can be difficult when emotions run high.

In the event that you're hoping something will workout without knowing how it's going to work out, that can be your first sign that something might be off and to start investigating.

Let me illustrate with a work example (it can be applied equally in personal situations).

I had an employee that was with my company from very early on. She was a superstar employee that drove a lot of successful results for the company. Fast forward a few years and her priorities in life had shifted and her performance suffered as a result, despite regular feedback. She was on the management team and this impacted the company morale.

However, given her loyalty to the business and past performance, I remained hopeful that things would somehow work out and that she'd revert to bringing back her A game. After things didn't change for over a year, I finally made the hard call to let her go and it turned out that she knew the decision was coming and was surprised that it didn't come sooner!

Some additional prompts:

-What's the challenge that I need to resolve?
-What solution makes sense?
-Am I feeling any doubts? If so, why?
-Am I ignoring any nagging voice inside my head?
-Do I have good reasons for making this decision? Am I too attached to this?

Going back to my previous situation, the answers would have been something like this:

What's the challenge that I need to resolve?

I need to improve the company's culture and not tolerate subpar performance.

What solution makes sense?

This person has been on the team for a long time and has a proven track record of being an A player. She just needs some more time to come back around.

Am I feeling any doubts? If so, why?

I feel some doubts because we've talked multiple times about her performance issues and she doesn't seem to be responding.

Do I have good reasons for making this decision? Am I too attached to this?

I think I'm too emotionally invested in the story that she's a core part of the company DNA and that the company just wouldn't be the same without her since she's also become a friend.

Whenever you feel any doubt, ask yourself, *Am I Attached? Am I letting my attachment obscure my vision of what's really going on? If so, what's really going on beneath the surface?*

WHO DO I TRUST?

Trust is the glue of life. It's the most essential ingredient in effective communication. It's the foundational principle that holds all relationships. — Stephen Covey

It's just so useful dealing with people you can trust and getting all the others the hell out of your life. It ought to be taught as a catechism. Wise people want to avoid other people who are just total rat poison, and there are a lot of them.
We try to operate in a web of seamless trust, deserved trust, and try to be careful whom we let in. — Charlie Munger

Having the right people in your life is one of the most important things that you can do. These are the people that will share your life journey with.

Spend a bit of time thinking about the people that you currently hangout with.

Then ask yourself, *Do I surround myself with people that I trust?*

With people that trust me? With people that have integrity?

You can think about specific situations such as:

Would I leave the keys to my home with this person for a few months?

Would I trust this person with my partner for a long period of time?

Would I trust this person with all of my money for a long period of time?

In order to trust in others, we must first be able to trust ourself.

Ask yourself, *Do I trust in myself?*

Do I consider myself trustworthy and deserving of trust?

Do I make and keep commitments? To myself and to others?

Do I keep my word?

AM I IN THE RIGHT RELATIONSHIP?

This is a useful question to ask yourself every now and then.

It's easy to get comfortable and attached to how things currently are. Don't let a decision you made without much thought a long time ago be the reason you *continue* to do something indefinitely. Just because you've always done something a certain way isn't a good reason to keep doing it that way. The best reason is because **it makes the most sense for you.**

Pay attention to the important areas of your life and give it a bit of time for reflection. Keep questioning the status quo.

You can substitute "relationship" for any area of life that you're considering.

Here are some examples to get you started:

Am I In The Right Relationship?
Am I In The Right Occupation?
Am I In The Right Company?
Am I In The Right Business?
Am I In The Right Industry?
Am I In The Right Country?

Don't stay in a relationship just because it's comfortable even though you don't see a future. It'll come to an end anyway so better to be fair to your partner and yourself, and have the courage to end it now than letting it drag on until you can't stand it anymore.

Don't stay in a job that you hate just because it pays the bill. Life's short so have the courage to go and figure out what it is that you actually want to do. That's not to say you'll find it straight away but at least you're on the path of discovery which will bring you closer to doing something you truly love.

The same can be said of the business you're running. Maybe you were passionate about the business at the beginning. But you've learned all you can from it, you've lost interest and now it's just paying the bills. It's okay to move on. Just because you are known as the successful software entrepreneur, doesn't mean you have to stay that same person forever. And just because you're a business owner, doesn't mean you have to stay a business owner forever. You can sell the business, change the direction of the business, give your company equity to your employees and let them run the show, shut it down, and so on.

Sometimes, people's interests change. Ed Thorp went from being a maths professor to hacking blackjack to a hedge fund manager to an author.

Other times, our interests stays the same. Warren Buffett has been investing since he was a teenager and it's still what he does today many, many decades later.

The point is to make sure that the path you're on is the one that you *continue* to choose.

Ask yourself, *Am I In The Right [Relationship/Career/Location]?*

PLAY

Life is like a play: it's not the length, but the excellence of the acting that matters — Seneca

WHAT'S THE ONE THING?

Before you start your day, ask yourself, *What's the one thing I can do that would make me feel happy with what I've done today?*

Another way to ask this is, *What is the most important thing that should be done today? What is the hardest thing that I need to do today? What would make today a win?*

Thinking about this question can help you avoid procrastinating important tasks indefinitely. It also prevents you from just being busy instead of being effective.

If you work in sales, it might be to reach out to 10 people today. If you're writing a book, it might be to write 10 pages. If your tax return is soon, then it's pushing that through.

When you do this first thing in the morning, you'll feel a sense of accomplishment and you'll feel momentum for the rest of your to-do list.

This can be done in view of a long term goal. For instance, it might to learn a programming language. Then the most important thing today can be spending one hour on a programming project.

For me to feel satisfied with the day, I like to have one thing that's **mentally challenging** and another thing that's **physically challenging**.

For the mentally challenging thing, some of the things I do include deep thinking about a particular question from this book, thinking through a programming problem, reading a physics textbook, and so on.

For the physically challenging thing, it can be running, uncomfortably long cold exposure after saunas, long walks, strenght training and so on.

Ask yourself at the start of the day, *What's The One Thing I Can Do To Make Today A Win?*

WHAT'S ONE POWERFUL BELIEF THAT I NEED TO ADOPT TODAY?

Never say never, because limits, like fears, are often just an illusion.
— Michael Jordan

Beliefs are powerful mechanisms that drive action, regardless of whether those underlying beliefs are true.

Thoughts create outcome.

Consider the 4 minute mile. Before it was broken, nobody thought it was possible.

After it was broken, it got broken regularly.

All it took was for one person to show that it's possible.

You can choose to believe that money is scarce or that money is everywhere. You can choose to believe in your own capabilities or you can choose to doubt yourself.

The beautiful thing is that **you can choose** which beliefs to adopt.

Ask yourself, *What's One Powerful Belief That I Need To Adopt Today?*

WHAT'S ONE THING I NEED TO STOP DOING IMMEDIATELY?

I'm actually as proud of the things we haven't done as the things I have done. Innovation is saying no to 1,000 things. — Steve Jobs

What's one thing that's preventing me from reaching my full potential?

From getting what I want?

Is it a distracting activity?

A destructive activity?

An activity that adds no value to my life?

WHO DO I NEED TO BE TO DO THIS?

Sometimes we know exactly what needs to be done.

But for whatever reason, we procrastinate.

Maybe it's a lack of motivation?
Maybe it's difficult?
Maybe it's unpleasant?

For those occasions, I find it helpful to put on a mask.

Kind of like when Bruce Wayne puts on his mask and becomes Batman. He becomes a different person.

A superhero that's capable of doing great things. Things that *need* to get done. Even if that thing happens to be difficult or unpleasant.

When you adopt the mask, you adopt the persona the mask represents.

And along with it, an amazing new capability to perform. To do what needs to get done.

Ask yourself, *Who do I need to be to do this?*

WHAT AM I TRYING TO AVOID?

Sometimes the very thing that we avoid tends to be the same thing that we need to do the most.

Spend some time to think about what you've been putting off.

If you're working in sales and you're procrastinating on generating leads because you don't want to pick up the phone, that's something you need to do first thing in the morning.

Maybe it's a difficult conversation with your partner about something you're not comfortable addressing but needs to be resolved.

Maybe you're dragging your feet on making an important decision.

Another way to look at this is to ask yourself, *Where am I pushing back? What am I resisting?*

The stronger the emotion, the stronger the tendency to procrastinate and to pushback.

Ask yourself, *What Am I Trying To Avoid?*

Prioritize the important items and you'll have a satisfying feeling of accomplishment.

IS THIS BINARY OR CONTINUOUS?

Let's say that you run a marketing team at a company.

You're not happy that the performance and you're not hitting the internal goals set.

You start to ask yourself, *Can I even manage a marketing team?*

Why isn't my marketing team performing?

Ask yourself, *Is this binary or continuous?*

You then realize that it's not a question of **IF** you can manage a marketing team (yes/no) but **HOW** good you are recruiting and managing a marketing team which falls on a scale of good to bad (continuum).

Now reframe your problem-based question into an outcome-based question.

You can ask yourself, *How Can I Make This An Empowering Question?*

Why isn't my marketing team performing? becomes *How do I learn to create a high-performance marketing team?*

Take a moment to reflect on how you might respond to both questions.

How do they differ?

A few examples of reframing:

Why isn't my business growing? becomes *How do I learn to create a growing business?*

Why am I not losing weight? becomes *How do I learn to create a system for losing weight?*

HOW CAN I MAKE THIS FEEL EASY?

You're stuck. You're procrastinating. Getting started seems daunting. Overwhelming. You put it off. Time just seems to fly.

Ask yourself, *How Can I Make This Feel Easy?*

Make it easy.

Make it accessible.

Look for the first step. Break it down to small, very easy to accomplish tasks.

Reading 10 books cover to cover sounds hard. Reading just one paragraph now or a book summary is easier.

Publishing a best selling book seems impossible. Writing the first page is easy.

Building a large software business seems difficult. Writing the first cold email to demo the software is easy.

Running a marathon seems out of reach. Jogging for 1 minute today is easy.

Look for the easy wins. Let the easy wins accumulate and gain momentum. The wins compound over time.

Don't make it difficult and complicated.

Don't make it such an enormous undertaking in your head that you never want to start.

Make it easier for yourself. Make it accessible.

Break down the things you want to do into easy, achievable steps. You've got this.

Start with the first step and ask yourself, *How Can I Make This Feel Easy?*

WHAT SHOULD I BE TRACKING?

What gets measured, gets managed — Peter Drucker

Pay attention to what you should be measuring by asking yourself, *What Should I Be Tracking?*

This starts with knowing what's important to you and the activities that you value.

When I wanted to lose weight, I got on the scale every morning right after waking up and logged the weight and the date. Of course, my weight would bounce up and down a lot as you might expect. But over time, my weight would start trending downward. By keeping an eye on my weight, I noticed small changes in my behavior. On days when the weight was more than I expected, then I might say to myself, *I can probably pass on this dessert for tonight.*

If you're already tracking something, then reflect on whether those metrics actually make sense for you.

All too often, we optimize for the wrong thing unintentionally and that can cause unintended behavior.

Is the focus sales or profit? Is it the number of books read or deep understanding of a particular topic? Is it losing body fat or building muscle? Is it growing the size of your network or increasing the depth of your existing connections?

If you're checking how many followers or how many likes you have on Instagram/TikTok/Snapchat many times throughout the day, your action is telling your brain that this is a metric that is important to you and you'll start optimizing for it, regardless of whether you've *consciously* decided it's important.

Think about whether it actually makes sense for you and see what else you're giving attention to during your day-to-day. Bring to surface the activities you're telling your mind is important and reflect on whether they really are important for you.

I keep track of the things that are important to me weekly, making each item on a scale of 1-10.

These include:
- Personal Relationships
  Physical Fitness
- Mental Fitness (how much I'm working my brain)
- Clean Eating
- Sleep/Rest
- Personal Development
- Whether I'm checking notifications too much

I'm a bit of a geek and will keep track of these on Google Sheets.

They help me keep in mind what I value and help me monitor how I'm doing over time.

The things that you track can change over time depending on your goals, where you're at in life, what you value, and so on.

Consider what's important for you and ask yourself, *What Should I Be Tracking?*

HOW CAN I DO THIS RIGHT?

Quidvis recte factum quamvis humile praeclarum (Whatever is rightly done, however humble, is noble) — Henry Royce

Everything we do matters. The small things. The big things.

The small things will usually be a good indicator of how we will end up doing the big things. If we do a terrible job at the small things, we'll most likely do it the same way with the bigger things too. As the old saying goes, *The way a person does one thing is the way they do everything.*

As you go about your work, ask yourself, *How Can I Do This Right? Am I Doing All That I Can? Have I Gone Above and Beyond?*

Whatever happens to be your job, do it well. Do it with pride. Do it with dedication.

If your job is one that you think is beneath you, that's going to show clearly with the way you do things, not only in your job.

Whatever your station currently is in life, fulfill your duties with grace.

Ask yourself, *How Can I Do This Right?*

RUI ZHI DONG

HOW CAN I DO THIS BETTER?

In everything we do, there's an opportunity.

A better way to do things.

Complacency is the enemy of excellence. It's easy to be complacent when we're no longer present and not fully engaged in the task at hand.

In your relationship, in your communication, in your work, in your daily routine — you will find an abundance of opportunities for improvement.

You can choose to work on just one thing to begin with and watch the changes compound over time.

Don't settle for good enough.

When Arnold Schwarzenegger was winning the bodybuilding contests, he'd still ask the judges at the end of each competition, *What were my weak points? What were my strong points?*

Think about the different areas of life where you can apply this.

It can be in the big things as well as the "little" things. Perhaps it's in the way you read a book. The way you take notes. The way you approach a work project. The way you go work out at the gym. The way you approach learning. The way you're handling constructive feedback.

A variation of this is, *Have I Given This Everything I've Got? Am I Doing All I Can? How Can I Produce Greater Results?*

There's always a way to do things better.

Ask yourself, *How Can I Do This Better?*

HOW CAN I DO THIS DIFFERENTLY?

The person who follows the crowd will usually go no further than the crowd. The person who walks alone is likely to find himself in places no one has ever seen before. — Albert Einstein

If something isn't working despite your best efforts, pause and reflect. Then try something different.

After all, Thomas Edison didn't try the *same* experiment 10,000 times. Instead, he learned from his previous experiments and tried something different. As Einstein's well-known saying goes, *insanity is doing the same thing over and over and expecting different results.*

Persistence is important. Persistence coupled with being open-minded and flexible is powerful.

Even when things are going your way, continue asking, *How Can I Do This Differently?*

Good advertisers will typically have a profitable base campaign and an experimental campaign that's always testing different creatives that might beat the base campaign.

When a new winner is found, that becomes the new base

campaign to beat. And so that process is repeated over and over again to produce better results.

What activities am I doing over and over again that I can do differently?

If you do the same thing as everyone else, you will produce average results.

Choose to be different. To think differently. Don't be afraid to be bold.

Ask yourself, *How Can I Do This Differently?*

HOW CAN I DO THIS BIGGER?

Think BIGGER.

Think, *How Can I 10x This? How would that look?*

How Can I Have The Absolute Maximum Possible Impact?

Where Are The Points of Leverage?

How Would This Look Scary Big?

We have a tendency to think small.

To avoid the feeling of failure.

To avoid being seen as a failure.

So we tend to stick with what seems safe and achievable.

I want to have interesting conversations with people wiser than myself and learn new things from them. The way I started is to approach the people I already knew.

Then I asked myself, *How Can I Do This Bigger?*

Perhaps one way of doing things *bigger* is to start a podcast or a YouTube channel.

So I decided to start a YouTube channel and share my conversations with the world.

I found that having the platform gave me the opportunity to have conversations with people I never imagined would have been possible as well as create something beautiful along the way. I've had very enjoyable conversations with people from all walks of life including with my favorite authors, with billionaire investors, and pretty much anyone that I found fascinating and wanted to learn from.

Imagine for a moment what you would attempt to do if you **knew for sure that you will not fail**.

Picture the capabilities that you would build along the way.

As the saying goes, *Shoot for the moon. Even if you miss, you'll land among the stars.*

Now imagine, *If there were no limitations at all, where would I shoot? What if I had all of the time and money that I needed? What if I already possessed all of the skills and knowledge required? What if I already have all of the self-belief and the self-confidence in abundance to succeed?*
The seemingly impossible is happening every day all around you.

What seemingly impossible outcomes will you create?

Dream on this.

Without any limitations.

Dwell on this picture.

Let your mind play this movie over and over again before you live them in reality.

WHERE DO I HAVE LEVERAGE?

We live in an age of infinite leverage. — Naval Ravikant

For most of human civilization, the input-output ratio of human activity has remained pretty constant.

If I spent 2 hours collecting tinder to make a fire, my output will not change dramatically. The 2 hours I put in would get me 2 hours of output.

Today through technological innovations, systems, capital, and cooperation, that's changed dramatically.

An idea on Kickstarter can raise millions.

A talented teacher in the middle of nowhere can educate the masses through YouTube.

A piece of code can impact billions of people.

Ask yourself, *Where Do I Have Leverage? What Are My Highest Leverage Activities? What Are My Force Multipliers? How Do I Create Leverage for the Outcomes That I Want?*

I find it helpful to think about the different categories of leverage to brainstorm ideas.

Leverage Through Tools

An axe is a force multiplier. It'd be difficult to get wood with only your barehands. Using an axe helps you magnify your effort so that you get more output.

Similarly, using Google Sheets with macros or automations is another force multiplier.

What tools am I already using that helps me achieve the outcomes I want? What other tools can I use?

Leverage Through Systems

Systems can be used to create outcomes on scale. Systems is how we get the same McDonald's burger whether you're in Mexico or Macedonia. What are systems? They're essentially just rules and repeatable processes to produce the results you want. The results can be electric cars, smartphones, and so on.

The outcome can also be intangible things like software, presentations, and ideas. I use a modified version of a note-taking system called *zettelkasten* together with powerful questions to consistently produce insights and creative ideas.

What systems can I adopt to create the outcomes I want?

Other Forms of Leverage

If you run a business, then one area of leverage is by training your staff. Let's say you spend 1 hour training a team of 20 people. Then those 20 people spend 40 hours implementing your idea.

That's a 1:800 ratio.

You can also gain leverage through capital by using someone else's money, either by them lending it to you or them investing it in you, which amplifies the outcome, both good and bad.

If you purchase a house on mortgage with a 10% deposit for instance, the bank has given you a leverage ratio of 1:10.

Ask yourself, *Where Do I Have Leverage?*

AM I OPERATING WITHIN MY ZONE OF GENIUS?

I'm no genius. I'm smart in spots — but I stay around those spots. — Tom Watson

Many of us like to think we're good at everything. But the truth of the matter is that we're usually very good at only a few things.

Figure out where you have an **edge**.

Warren Buffett calls it his *circle of competence*. He sticks with investing in companies that operates in industries he truly understands.

Having the self awareness of knowing where your core strength lay will set you apart from the crowd.

Stay within your zone of genius. **Focus**.

The name of the game is not about expanding your zone. It's about having the awareness of knowing where your circle is and operating within it. That's how you play to win.

So ask yourself, *Am I Operating within My Zone of Genius?*

HOW DO I DESERVE THIS?

Karma is just you, repeating your patterns, virtues, and flaws until you finally get what you deserve. — Naval Ravikant

We want the best in life. The best house. The best income. The best spouse. The best career. The best business. The best friends. The best life.

The key question to ask yourself is, *How Do I Deserve This?*

People that win lotteries rarely keep the money they win. Most end up with the same net worth they had before they won. They won the money through sheer luck. They didn't earn it and they couldn't handle the money.

The same goes with relationships. You want to be with someone amazing — beautiful, smart, funny, generous, caring. Yet, what have you done to deserve it? Become the person that deserves to be in a relationship with the person of your dreams. That always starts with **working on yourself.**

Whether in relationships, career, business, or wealth, the growth that you see is typically a reflection of someone's personal growth. Someone that's grown a business from $1 million a year to $10 million a year has themselves grown in the process by **becoming the person their business needs them to be in order to grow**.

Whenever I hear myself say, *I want X*, it automatically triggers my next response, *How Do I Deserve This?*

I want to write a book. *How Do I Deserve This?* Start with writing one page a day instead of just talking about it.

I want to be a successful value investor. *How Do I Deserve This?* Start with reading every book I can find on value investing.

I want to have a lot of money. *How Do I Deserve This?* Start with thinking about how you can add value or contribute to the world.

I want to have a muscular body. *How Do I Deserve This?* Start with working out consistently at the gym.

I want to be a YouTube influencer. *How Do I Deserve This?* Start with making videos consistently.

WHICH FIRE DO I ALLOW TO CONTINUE BURNING?

Picture an emergency room surgeon trying to save the life of a trauma patient; as she's conducting emergency surgery, she might notice a suspicious-looking mass, but she's going to focus on patching the patient's arteries first — there will be time for biopsies and tests later. After all, if the patient dies on the operating table, even a potential tumour will be irrelevant. — Reid Hoffman

When there are many fires to put out, we may not have the time or resources to deal with all of them at once.

We must prioritize the biggest fires first and let the rest burn in the meantime.

In the early days of PayPal when they were growing rapidly, they couldn't handle the surge of customer service tickets. Angry customers started calling because they weren't getting replies. The issue was that PayPal also had many, even *bigger* problems to deal with.

So they decided just to stop picking up the phones altogether while they put out the biggest fires first.

If you're dealing with many fires, don't run to put out the fire you happen to encounter.

Take a step back and look at the bigger picture.

By solving one problem, you may let a different problem become truly threatening.

Be strategic.

Ask yourself, *Which Fire Do I Allow To Continue Burning?*

HOW CAN I OVERCOME THIS?

When you're exhausted, weak, and tired and everyone around you looks just as bad as you or even worse — that's the perfect time for you to make a statement. You let everyone around you know that when their life ends, that's when yours begins. — David Goggins

We're faced with obstacles all the time. Consider them an opportunity to demonstrate your strength of character by overcoming it. A test of your resolve.

When things are not working out, it's easy to run away. When we're pushing at our limits physically, the body wants to give up. People will tell you that what you're trying to achieve is impossible.

Don't accept the limitations. They limit your reality.

Greatness is achieved from within.

The next time you confront an obstacle, ask yourself, *How Can I Overcome This?*

WHAT'S THE TRUE COST OF THIS?

We must all suffer one of two things: the pain of discipline or the pain of regret. — Jim Rohn

It's easy to start doing things mindlessly. For example, once you start watching Netflix, you might unwittingly binge watch an entire season in one sitting.

During the activity in question, ask yourself, *What's the True Cost of This?*

When we think about the cost of things, whether in terms of money or time, it's too abstract for the brain.

State the response instead in terms of something that you find valuable.

Instead of answering, 5 hours, I would say, *The true cost of watching this Netflix series is one life changing book.*

Other things include spending time with loved ones, mastering the basics of a language, learning something cool, time in the sauna, dinner with friends, getting a massage, sleep, and so on. Choose the activities that click with you. It doesn't need to stay the same over time.

This is not to say that one activity is better than the other. It's to stay conscious of what you value by stating the alternative things you could be doing and not mindlessly doing things that you didn't intend to and don't value.

If you're looking to spend less time on a particular activity, this is a useful prompt. It's easy to get drawn into activities unwittingly, and then to take it to excess.

Ask yourself, *What is the True Cost Of This?*

Use the opportunity to moderate or altogether eliminate the activity that you don't value a lot.

Another approach is to consider substitutes.

Instead of mindlessly scrolling on social media, send someone a thoughtful note.

HOW CAN I LEAVE THE WORLD A BETTER PLACE?

To leave the world a bit better, whether by a healthy child, a garden patch, or a redeemed social condition; to know that even one life has breathed easier because you have lived — that is to have succeeded.
— Ralph Waldo Emerson

The meaning of life is to find your gift. The purpose of life is to give it away. — Pablo Picasso

When I think about this question, the first thing I think of is, *How Do I Avoid Making The World Worse Off?*

After that, I'll reflect on the question, *What Should I Contribute?*

I think about the things that bring me joy, the areas where I have particular strength, and where I can make a difference.

WHAT ARE THE MOST IMPORTANT QUESTIONS?

For pretty much every aspect of life, there are powerful questions to be asked that can help you gain clarity, uncover insights, understand yourself, avoid making stupid decisions, and more.

Make it a habit to ask yourself, *What's the better question here? How can I find the better question?*

If you ask yourself often enough, it becomes a powerful muscle.

Even for the seemingly simple day to day activities, the right questions can help you be more effective and more focused.

While I'm writing, I might think about the following:

-Who am I writing for?
-What am I writing about?
-What's the main point that I'm trying to make?

When I'm reading:

-What kind of book is this? This will change the way you read

and perceive the book.
-What is the book trying to argue and how does the structure of the book help the author convey that argument?
-What's the main question that the book is trying to answer?

Whether in your day to day activities or in the bigger picture, look for the better question to ask.

What are the unasked questions?

What are questions that I should be asking but not asking?

What questions am I too afraid to ask?

Courage doesn't happen when you have all the answers. It happens when you are ready to face the questions you have been avoiding your whole life. — Shannon L. Alder

Asking the better questions will lead to better answers.

What are the big questions that currently drive your life?

CONCLUSION

I very much enjoy hearing from my readers and if there are any particular power questions that have made an impact on you, please let me know about them :)

If you have found this book to be helpful or insightful, I would be incredibly grateful if you could take a moment to leave a review on Amazon. I would love to hear about your thoughts, your journey, and any insights you've discovered about yourself! What you write will help others on similar journeys and looking for answers.

For those interested in connecting, please feel free to send me an email at rui@ruizhidong.com :)

Printed in Great Britain
by Amazon